THE EROTIC SPACE AROUND ART OBJECTS

PREVIOUSLY BY EILEEN R. TABIOS

POETRY

After The Egyptians Determined The Shape of the World Is A Circle, 1996
Beyond Life Sentences, 1998
The Empty Flagpole (CD with guest artist Mei-mei Berssenbrugge), 2000
Ecstatic Mutations (with short stories and essays), 2001
Reproductions of The Empty Flagpole, 2002
Enheduanna in the 21st Century, 2002
There, Where the Pages Would End, 2003
Menage a Trois With the 21st Century, 2004
Crucial Bliss Epilogues, 2004
The Estrus Gaze(s), 2005
Songs of the Colon, 2005
Post Bling Bling, 2005
I Take Thee, English, For My Beloved, 2005
The Secret Lives of Punctuations, Vol. I, 2006
Dredging for Atlantis, 2006
It's Curtains, 2006
SILENCES: The Autobiography of Loss, 2007
The Singer and Others: Flamenco Hay(na)ku, 2007
The Light Sang As It Left Your Eyes: Our Autobiography, 2007
Nota Bene Eiswein, 2009
Footnotes to Algebra: Uncollected Poems 1995-2009, 2009
On A Pyre: An Ars Poetica, 2010
Roman Holiday, 2010
Hay(na)ku for Haiti, 2010
THE THORN ROSARY: Selected Prose Poems and New 1998-2010, 2010
the relational elations of ORPHANED ALGEBRA (with j/j hastain), 2012
5 Shades of Gray, 2012
THE AWAKENING: A Long Poem Triptych & A Poetics Fragment, 2013
147 Million Orphans (MMXI-MML), 2014
44 RESURRECTIONS, 2014
SUN STIGMATA (Sculpture Poems), 2014
I Forgot Light Burns, 2015
Duende in the Alleys, 2015
INVENT(ST)ORY: Selected Catalog Poems & New (1996-2015), 2015
The Connoisseur of Alleys, 2016
The Gilded Age of Kickstarters, 2016
Excavating the Filipino in Me, 2016
I Forgot Ars Poetica, 2016
AMNESIA: Somebody's Memoir, 2016
THE OPPOSITE OF CLAUSTROPHOBIA: Prime's Anti-Autobiography, 2017
Post-Ecstasy Mutations, 2017
On Green Lawn, The Scent of White, 2017
To Be An Empire Is To Burn, 2017
If They Hadn't Worn White Hoods ... (with John Bloomberg-Rissman), 2017
What Shivering Monks Comprehend, 2017
YOUR FATHER IS BALD: Selected Hay(na)ku Poems, 2017
IMMIGRANT: Hay(na)ku & Other Poems In A New Land, 2017
Comprehending Mortality (with John Bloomberg-Rissman), 2017
Big City Cante Intermedio, 2017
WINTER ON WALL STREET: A Novella-in-Verse, 2017
Making National Poetry Month Great Again, 2017
MANHATTAN: An Archaeology, 2017
Love In A Time of Belligerence, 2017
MURDER DEATH RESURRECTION: A Poetry Generator, 2018
TANKA, Vol. I, 2018
HIRAETH: Tercets From The Last Archipelago, 2018
One, Two, Three: Selected Hay(na)ku Poems (Trans. Rebeka Lembo), 2018
THE GREAT AMERICAN NOVEL: Selected Visual Poetry 2001-2019, 2019
The In(ter)vention of the Hay(na)ku: Selected Tercets 1996-2019, 2019 & 2021
Witness in the Convex Mirror, 2019
Evocare: Selected Tankas (with Ayo Gutierrez and Brian Cain Anne), 2019
We Are It, 2020
Inculpatory Evidence: The Covid-19 Poems, 2020
Political Love, 2021
La Vie érotique de l'art, une séance avec William Carlos Williams (Trad. de l'anglais (États-Unis) par Samuel Rochery), 2021
PRISES (Trad. de l'anglais (États-Unis) par Fanny Garin), 2022
Because I Love You, I Become War, 2023
Drawing the Six Directions, 2024
Engkanto in the Diaspora, 2025

FICTION

Behind The Blue Canvas, 2004
Novel Chatelaine, 2009
SILK EGG: Collected Novels 2009-2009, 2011
What Counts, 2020
PAGPAG: The Dictator's Aftermath in the Diaspora, 2020
DOVELION: A Fairy Tale for Our Times, 2021
Simmering: a novella-in-prose-poems, 2022
Getting to One, flash fictions with art by harry k stammer, 2023
KalapatingLeon (Trans. into Filipino by Danton Remoto), 2024
The Balikbayan Artist, 2024
Tata Efren's Forever Laughter, with Mel Vera Cruz and Jeannie M. Celestial, 2026
The Erotic Space Around Art Objects, 2026

PROSE COLLECTIONS

Black Lightning: Poetry-In-Progress (poetry essays/interviews), 1998
My Romance (art essays with poems), 2002
The Blind Chatelaine's Keys (biography with haybun), 2008
AGAINST MISANTHROPY: A Life in Poetry (2015-1995), 2015
#EileenWritesNovel, 2017
Tiny Stickers: A Covid-19 Autobiography, 2020
THE INVENTOR: A Poet's Transcolonial Autobiography, 2023

THE EROTIC SPACE AROUND ART OBJECTS

Selected Art Stories (1996-2026)
by Eileen R. Tabios

Art by harry k stammer

Sandy Press

Cover design, art & interior layout by
harry k stammer

ISBN: 979-8-9924582-9-9

Printed in U.S.A.

Sandy Press

http://sandy-press.com

Author's and Artist's Notes

I love art: I feel that paintings, sculptures and drawings speak, and I feel blessed that some choose to reveal their tales to me. The stories in this collection were inspired by the creations of the following visual artists and objects, as follows:

"About Face": Gustave Courbet, Brice Marden
"Ant-ish Lesson": Leonardo da Vinci (who the author imagines could have invented the fictional MV Pot-Belly Rocket)
"The Art Collector": Jeff Burton, Exeias, Michelle O'Connor, Phidias, Richard Thatcher, Richard Tsao
"The Artist Looks at the Model": anonymous Greek sculptor of "The Kritios Boy" (circa 480 B.C.)
"Bar-Hopping Sentences": The Peacekeeper American Bourbon Whiskey for its bottle that's shaped like a mobile ICBM missile
"Blue Richard": René Magritte and various Native American potters and weavers
"Brutality": Phidias, who guided the Greek sculptors who created the Parthenon Marbles during 5th century BC
"The Caustic Surface": Richard Hogan, Wassily Kandinsky, Eadward Muybridge, Sonita Singwi, Li Ti, Eleanore Weber, Wang Wei
"Einstein's Love Story": Osami Tanaka
"The First Poetry Book": Frida Kahlo, Fernando Amorsolo
"La Luna 'Before Silence Comes'": Theresa Chong, Jackson Pollock, Mark Rothko, James Westwater
"Letter to a Newly-Lapsed Nun & Other Philosophers": Leonardo da Vinci
"Non-Fungible Armadillo Shells": Mike Winkelmann aka Beeple
"One Eye Open": the makers of ancient Greek coins featuring dolphin-riders used in Taras founded in 8th century BC, now known as Taranto in Italy
"The 'Other'": Gustave Courbet, Richard Serra

“Polmost Spirytus Rektyfikowany Vodka”: The Toltecs (of pre-Columbian Mesoamerican culture) who built the Temple of Kukulcan in the Chichen Itza archeological site of Yucatan, Mexico
“Red ‘Afterbirth’”: Richard Tuttle

—Eileen R. Tabios

The engravings function as a deliberate diversion. They are meant to draw attention away from the book’s stated visual-art inspirations rather than reinforce them. They do not correspond to the artists or artworks mentioned, nor do they operate as secondary or derivative inspirations drawn from the author’s own sources. Their role is non-relational and interruptive—an intentional visual interference. Like the persistent speck in a Francis Bacon painting, it keeps pulling the eye away from what appears to be the subject, resisting coherence and discouraging easy readings of influence.

—harry k stammer

CONTENTS

Engraving 1

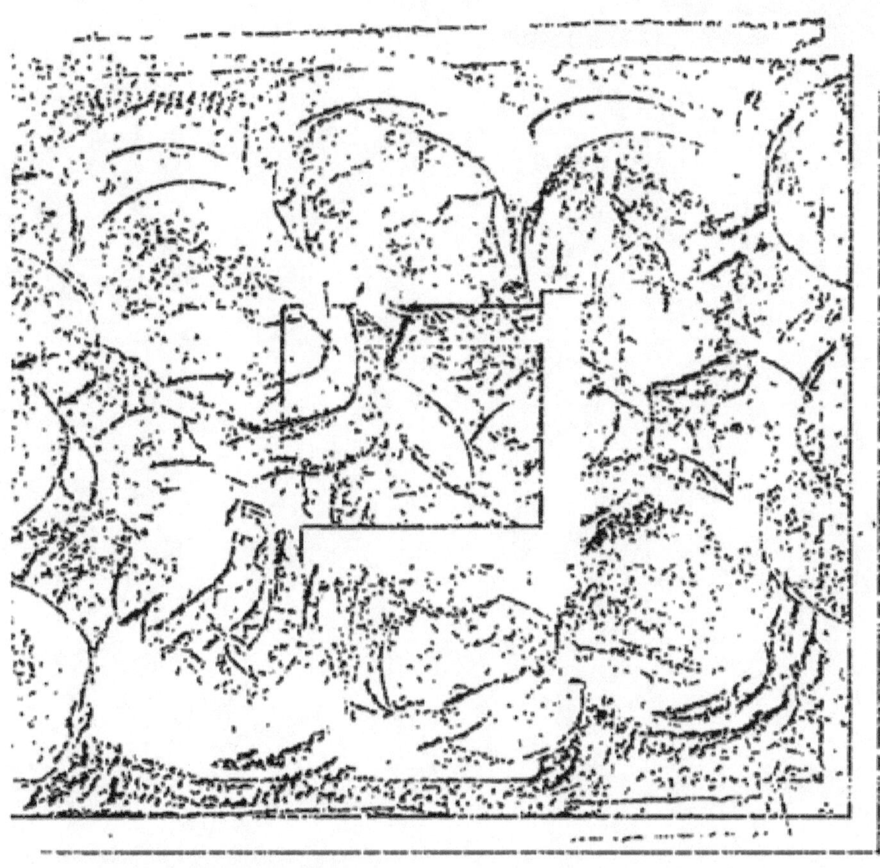

I. EKPHRASTIC TALES

Her face is so clear
that when you gaze
on its perfections

you see your own face
reflected.
—from "White Skin" by Ibn 'Abd Rabbihi

Red "Afterbirth"

> *Even this very act of tracing words on paper in order to arrest the expediency of not remembering constitutes a polemic whose expositions and explications have, as their sole purpose, that of convincing myself that this tale's elements, in their intensity and extent, are contained in my own history.*
> ***—from "Identifications" by Clinton Palanca***

Manila, several years ago:

In the beginning, I thought to dissuade him because I thought him only a boy. But the sun's red stain on his cheeks made me linger, made me feel the sun wish to implode to continue caressing the flesh pulled tightly over his angled cheekbones. Later, I would hear from others in his village that his complexion was considered unusual. The sun never darkened him, only deepened the ruddiness on his skin until it evoked an ember of coal flickering its last breaths. Then he pushed up his sleeves and his forearms made me pause. In that moment, too, I noticed other muscles rippling under the weak camouflage of a thin shirt. The first time I looked into his eyes, I heard a radio come to life and a woman start to whisper, *I forgot the horizon is far, is near, is what you wish but always in front of you.*

I forgot one can choose always to face the horizon ... He spoke slowly but I couldn't understand a word, hearing only the whispered song and a faint buzzing. I looked towards the open door, expecting to see bees inebriated with pollen. A dryness in my throat, I let Mama deal with him and walked away. Mama asked him to stay for dinner. I don't know what I would have done if she hadn't. Perhaps I would have stopped, turned and been the one to ask him to stay for dinner. Perhaps I would have kept walking as I did towards my studio in the garden. Later he would tell me that he watched a strand of my hair fall as I left, that he watched it slowly coil itself over the back of a chair and that he picked it up when Mama wasn't looking.

The canvas on my easel heightened my restlessness. It hadn't yet immobilized my hand, and I reached once more for the brush. When I looked at it again after two hours, the green strokes were completely obliterated by swaths of blood red stains. Mama was calling me into the house for dinner. As I walked through the kitchen door, I said I needed to wash myself clean of the paint. I could feel the paint clinging to my hands, my arms, like lovers' palms reluctant to let go. Mama said Noel was taking a nap on my bed as he had driven all day to bring news from my grandmother. That's how I choose to recall first hearing his name, "Noel"—in the context of his sinking onto my bed, his hair falling against my pillow and his eyes seeing what I, too, see when I lie back on my bed: a sketch I once drew of a desert's infinite expanse, the limb of a cactus plant on the foreground and the moon tiny but undeniably full in the distance of background.

THE NEXT TIME I ALLOWED HIM ON MY BED, I MOSTLY HAD MY EYES CLOSED. I OPENED THEM ONLY WHEN FINALLY I LOST ALL CONTROL.

I told Mama I'd wake Noel. In the hallway bathroom, I ran my hands under the faucet and thought of blood and afterbirth while the water gathered in the sink. When my hands were clear once more, I looked at myself in the mirror. I placed my wet palms against my cheeks, but the fever remained. I wanted to commit an act of violence. I wanted this same urge to abate. But Mama called once more. So I went to where he laid on my bed.

I closed the door behind me as I stepped into my bedroom. I let the dimness fall like a cloak as I walked to where he slept. He had taken off his shirt. A streetlamp flickered beyond the window and lit where he lay. My left hand rose to betray me and slowly reached for him. I felt the heat from his skin but before I could touch him, he opened his eyes. I thought to draw back but he immediately raised his torso to meet my hand. "Your name is sweet," he said as my hand recoiled from his warm flesh. "No," I said. He knew I meant something else when I said, "My name is Rose."

I crushed garlic and dropped them in vinegar and salt. I liked dipping Mama's vegetable egg rolls in this make-shift sauce. He kept complimenting Mama over her beef sauteed with mushrooms and spinach, her crisply fried chicken, her pork simmered with eggplants in a fish sauce and her barbecued ribs. I arranged and rearranged the few pieces on my plate while he seemed inexhaustible. Mama was vibrating in delight at his fulsome appetite and compliments. He only looked at me once, at the end of the meal. He didn't hide the hunger still simmering in his eyes.

Mama offered him the living room sofa for the night. I didn't offer my bedroom, although I planned to sleep in my studio that night. I planned to paint over the canvas waiting for me. I wanted to paint over the red. When he asked to see my studio, Mama eagerly jumped in, "That's a good idea, Rose. It would be nice to get another person's opinion." I muttered, "Why?" But Mama didn't hear me. He did and merely smiled.

WHEN I LOSE CONTROL, HE SMILES. THEN HE MAKES ME LOSE CONTROL AGAIN.

The painting mocked me as soon as we entered the studio. "The paint is wet," he observed. "I'm still working on it. It's not finished yet," I said. He raised an eyebrow and gestured towards the mattress against the wall. "I'll just sit there and watch. Don't let me get in the way." I wanted to tell him to leave but shrugged instead. I turned back to the painting, even as I felt him drop to where I had slumbered for a few hours earlier that day.

I reached for a brush, then stopped my hand in mid-air. "Name me," the painting ordered. It was done. For the first time, I tried to fight against the work and railed back, "Not yet!" This dialogue must have taken but a few seconds and in silence. But

Noel was immediately by my side, clasping my bereft hand left clutching at air. "It's flawed, but perfectly so," he said.

My hair fell loose from where I had pinned them. I snatched back my hand and kept shaking until he used his palms to still my face. We looked at each other like this for a long time.

Finally, I whispered, "I am much older than you." He placed his lips on my cheek, just barely touching the corner of my lips. He whispered back, "By a year?" Because I felt him silently laugh, I didn't explain.

WHEN I LOSE CONTROL, HE SMILES. THEN HE MAKES ME LOSE CONTROL AGAIN. ONCE, HE SAID HE LOVED TO WATCH ME OPEN MY EYES TO HIS WATCH.

He's in New York now, attending the Art Students League. He is a sculptor, but I didn't know this until it was too late. I thought he was just a farmer who would return to a village I had never seen and did not anticipate visiting in the future, as later I would in an attempt to recreate him in my mind. When I asked, he said, "I like sculpting air into what I feel because air is stubborn and makes me question, too, what I feel. I like the process of achieving certainty."

I had left New York after my first solo show at one of the city's most prestigious galleries. I received rave reviews, and my dealer sold everything from the show. She wanted more of my paintings, but she said, "I want more of the same as we hung in your show. Extend this series. I can sell whatever you produce." I couldn't have obeyed her, even if I had wanted to, even if I hadn't taken a left turn and veered off the road. Even if I hadn't veered off the road, I would have wanted to go explore.

Certainty is an ambitious goal, I thought, but decided to remain silent. I was distracted, too, by my hands' betrayal. Pressed against his chest, they began to seek, aching to feel what I only had sensed behind fragile cloth. He didn't move, his palms still holding my face as he watched me breathe through parted lips. Finally, my hands opened a button and reached for the skin over his heart. At the touch of my fingers where his heart beat, he whispered, "I have always known you."

My mother and his mother were best friends during their high school days in the Philippines. My mother renewed their acquaintance when she left the United States to retire in Manila. Mama showed them catalogues of my paintings when they visited her. He said he admired everything he saw, but was most appreciative of my progression as he tracked my works over time. He said, "I like the way you think."

Through the Art Students League, he obtained a student visa to go to New York. I told him about my former dealer. The first time he wrote after leaving me in Manila, a year had passed, and he enclosed a catalogue my former dealer put together for his first show. He also said his art requires him to remain in the city I had left.

The catalogue showed he had created eight sculptures, each

comprised of a single black rope interacting in angled patterns against the gallery's white walls. All began from a point nailed against the wall, then looped around several nails before ending under a nail piercing the floor in front of the wall. The catalogue's photos showed the shadows the ropes cast, and which became integrated into the works. The pieces were all titled, "Rose" with the numbers "1" to "8" after my name to differentiate one from the other. In the note he enclosed with the catalogue, he wrote, "The first time we met, you turned your back on me. And a single strand of hair separated itself from your receding presence. When I picked it up, it clung to me. It clings to me still."

WHEN I LOSE CONTROL, HE SMILES. THEN HE MAKES ME LOSE CONTROL AGAIN. ONCE, HE SAID HE LOVED TO WATCH ME OPEN MY EYES TO HIS WATCH. ONCE, I ASKED, ARE YOU ALWAYS SO CONTROLLED?

It might as well be yesterday.

~~

<u>Manila, today:</u>

Mama visited New York last month and returned bearing a catalogue from his latest and fifth show. "Isn't it sweet of him to name his works after you?" Mama asked. The numbers were "45" to "57." But this time, the ropes were stained dark red, like the color of blood after it has congealed. In the letter he sent with my mother, he wrote, “I have these dreams of sculptures formed from the soil where your studio stands. I think, with the right chemicals, they can create a compound like clay. And I want to mold them with my bare hands after my bare hands have done something else. Are you still there? I am no longer a boy.” It was his second letter, and it had been several years since he left Manila.

After reading his letter the first time, easily memorizing all of it with that one perusal, I raised my eyes from the words his heart felt, his mind created, and his hands physically formed on paper. I looked at the red canvas hanging by the door in my studio. I changed its title from "Wound" to "Afterbirth."

He arrives tomorrow. I am convinced it might as well be yesterday. Today, I work with the color green, like the clean leaves in the garden sparkling after a storm or the tears of a gentle rain.

WHEN I LOSE CONTROL, HE SMILES. THEN HE MAKES ME LOSE CONTROL AGAIN. ONCE, HE SAID HE LOVED TO WATCH ME OPEN MY EYES TO HIS WATCH. ONCE, I ASKED, ARE YOU ALWAYS SO CONTROLLED? HE TOOK HIS TIME REPLYING, ISN'T CONTROL PART OF BEING CERTAIN?

The green paint works easily with me, even as I think about other things besides my hand wielding the brush. I am certain I will love the result, though I don't yet know whether I will end up layering it with random flicks of paints from other colors—a thought I am still only turning over in my mind. It doesn't matter when the artist destroys an image. When an image is obsessive, it will reappear. When an image is forgotten, then and only then can it become a Muse.

In response, I wrote Noel that, in Manila, I still waited. I said:

> *An immediate experience is without value unless the essence of that experience already has germinated within the artist's mind. On each end of a relationship, anyone can react to a scene of an accident without necessarily understanding its cause. "La mesure humaine" defines the equation between an art object and the dimension of man. The difference between dimensions is optics. Before artists destroyed perspective, the proper scale for a painting was determined without any concessions to peripheral vision, unlike sculptures that require the viewer to move physically, retaining previous impressions in memory as momentum continues. History prevents space from becoming a void. There are questions to be answered in how to evolve a wall into a window. What surfaces will be the result of perfect alignment.*

Beyond the open door, I noticed that the moon was a perfectly rounded pearl against the ebony sky, and that the sky remained perfectly still even as the Milky Way shifted. My lips parted as I concluded my letter, “Alignment is a paradoxical relationship between life and the space that life inhabits.”

La Luna "Before Silence of Winter Comes"

When I met him, I was looking at a scarlet moon. Midnight was still mere fiction.

Virgin moons are swathed in blood. They first appear suffused in red, the longest wave light emanating from the spectrum of the sun as it sinks beneath the horizon. As night matures and the moon reaches for the stars, *la luna* whitens. Since I preferred the radiance of a ruby to the self-effacement of a pearl, I considered the moon's nightly cycle as emblematic of time's dangerous potential for diluting the spirit. After all, life is not easy.

"You don't know what you're doing but you will. You've got great guts," he said as I looked at "La Luna Naranja," the largest work in the front room of the 7th Boulevard Gallery. The red-orange moon was a circle whose edges touched four sides of the 68" X 68" canvas. I was communing with my paintings as the show was scheduled to end the following day. I turned towards the confident voice, mentally leaving Mojacar, Spain where I first saw an infant moon.

I was insulted, having memorized *The Weekly Villager*'s brief but rave review of my first solo show. I held back from flagellating him with my eyes only because he immediately introduced himself. At its utterance, his name seemed to become tangible and hang within the few inches of air that separated us: Jason Yardley. He had cut his hair since he posed for last month's *ART EXPOSED*. But his eyes remained as green as they were on the cover of the country's leading art magazine: a dark green like the dimness of underbrush, a green like a lament, a green like a sonata.

I also noticed his height. I felt my chin lift as I tried to see what else lurked within his eyes besides the color green. But the gesture made me lean towards his lips and, awkwardly, I stepped back. He noticed, but the star of 57th Street's most prestigious gallery cast his eyes at the moon behind me. Still, he disconcerted me more with the courtesy of his act so that I could recover equilibrium without the press from his eyes.

His gallery MB Inc. was managed by Mindy "Witch" Babson. She attained her nickname for trying to emulate the critic Clement Greenberg by telling artists what and how to paint. She also busily promoted something she called "Formal Gesturalism," diligently searching for painters she could include in this "innovative school" regardless of whether her targeted artists had thought at all about her premise of "flat color fields depicted by elongated brushstrokes that logically extended art into the next century by breaking down borders between passion and dispassion."

As the Witch frequently touted to those in the art media with whom she long enjoyed an incestuous relationship borne of free paintings and the generous use of her bed, Jason's works exemplified Formal Gesturalism in the same way Andy Warhol's exemplified Pop Art. But as Jason told *ART EXPOSED's* interviewer, he just painted what he wished and how others interpreted his paintings was not his concern. In the next paragraph, the interviewer described Jason as "possessing a delectable sense of humor." This, the interviewer attributed to Jason grinning while he noted, "Besides, Mindy's got the kind of clientele that quickly pushes artists' prices to six figures and, hey, I'm not one to complain. She can call my works whatever she wants as long as she sells them."

I wanted to show I wasn't impressed by *THE* Jason Yardley and blurted, "Oh? You still know what 'guts' are?"

We looked at each other as the significance of my statement surfaced like a nose-crunching stench. Unintentionally, I had referenced the recent controversy over his works—that he was turning out too many paintings of the same type rather than continuing to develop. One wag even joked that Jason Yardley was no longer painting but just managing an assembly line from his studio in Galisteo, New Mexico. Since his works were sized no larger than 36" X 36" and offered images of single lines curving across single-color backgrounds, it was easy for the joke to spread. It was particularly popular with those mindful of Mindy Babson's growing power, a potential that seemed poised to rival Mary Boone's influence on the 1980s New York art scene.

Flustered, I offered, "I'm sorry. I didn't mean to insult you."

"No, don't apologize. I'll just choose to be flattered you've even thought of me," he said, after a quizzical look.

Then, clearly deciding to bear no grudge, he grinned—but the lightening of his countenance only made me realize he was just a few years older. It was a depressing revelation, highlighting how long it had taken me to have my first solo show. Unlike MB Inc., my small gallery was patronized mostly by other emerging artists who were too poor to acquire works even though they were priced at a fraction of the cost of their materials.

The 7th Boulevard Gallery was managed on a cooperative basis by twelve painters whose "day jobs" allowed them to split its operating costs. For all of us, it was the only space where we could show our works beyond the occasional representation in some group show sponsored by galleries who were usually as obscure as ours. The 7th Boulevard Gallery's artists even took turns playing "Vassar Girl"—what we called the art world's black-clad women and men who sat behind a desk with brochures and price lists to answer questions that visitors may pose about the exhibits.

"You've got great guts," Jason repeated. "Come to MB Inc. this evening. I'm opening a show."

He looked at "La Luna Naranja" once more, then left.

Larry, that month's Vassar Girl, was entering as Jason was leaving. He did a double-take, caught my eye and gestured, "Wasn't that . . .?"

"Yes," I interrupted. "The big kahuna himself, in town for his latest and much-anticipated show at MB Inc. He said I didn't know what I'm doing."

"What?"

Larry dashed over and began fussing over my unique use of foreground, the colors only I could mix, and so on. I shushed him and motioned towards a couple across the room who were perusing the price list. As this implied, they could be interested in purchasing a painting, Larry reluctantly left me for them. I couldn't be bothered to explain that Jason Yardley didn't mean to insult me. I was already looking at my paintings with fresh eyes. That's when I realized that my colors were too lush, too brilliant. Visually, their robustness made them instantly accessible to the viewer who could marvel over the colors which I concocted with pride. But they seemed two-dimensional, failing my desire to offer a way for intriguing the intellect: my paintings were like adorable infants, extending their flailing arms for hugs as they babbled words that enchanted but had no meaning.

~~

"Atom-size objects move in jerky leaps from one place to another without signs of the travel between—so-called 'quantum jumps'—meaning no one can predict just where an object is going to be," the Witch was proclaiming as I stepped through her gallery's doors. As I walked past the group dotted with fur-clad collectors, her eyes cut sideways at my scuffed workman's boots.

Because her glance dismissed me, I walked past them even though Jason stood in their midst. I could feel his eyes track me as the Witch continued, "The second idea is that tiny objects cannot exist, independent of its observers. In the act of observation these tiny objects take on characteristics that would not have been present before they were observed. By looking for one feature of an object, one completely alters the object's other features in unpredictable ways. Thus, what one chooses to examine alters what exists."

I was stopped by a waiter who offered me a tray with glasses of wine and water. I opted for water *con gas* as I heard Jason add, "The third idea is that there has to be a new order in the universe, despite the apparent disorder presented by the first two ideas. This order is not the order expected based on classical physics—instead it's an order that involves us. It involves our minds in a way that we couldn't have expected using the old physics. This order suggests that we are in control of possibilities but not actualities."

Geeezz! People talk like that to each other? I looked around the room but saw no one I recognized. I began pacing along the walls, looking at his paintings. The first thing I noticed was that he'd expanded his scale. All were at least as large as my "La Luna Naranja." Each work featured a luminous field of yellow crossed by inch-wide lines of black curving from one edge to another adjacent edge. Each also had a tiny red dot pasted on the wall beside them indicating the Witch had sold out another show.

"You look great," he whispered into my hair. I hadn't noticed him come toward me. I immediately tore into myself for wearing my red velvet dress. I thought it would look cool to pair it with my work boots. But, just then, I felt like a modern-day version of Miss Kitty from the prior century's cowboy-popcorn, "Gunsmoke."

"I'm sure you look better," I said, then hated myself for attempting to be flippant.

"How would you know if you don't look?" he teased. I could feel sunlit days lurking beneath his light tone. He placed a palm on each shoulder and turned me around to look at him. I could feel the laughter he stored behind his impassive face. He was dressed in a black suit over a shirt so white it seemed like a lightning bolt against a night sky. But as I stared at him, the black and white contrast dislodged another memory: a thin waterfall deeply recessed into a cliff—a sight I once saw from a lake in Hawai'i and which so tempted me that I had paddled my canoe towards it. I remembered resting behind the waterfall, watching it glisten in front of me, its white light occasionally interrupted by fragments of a rainbow—I remembered just sitting there, grinning foolishly. For years afterwards, I had felt that afternoon to have been the peak of happiness until the moment I stepped back from "La Luna Naranja" and considered my painting done.

I swallowed as I dropped my eyes and kept them fixed on his shirt collar. My eyes ached to travel to a pulse beating near where his top button laid unfastened. But I tried to avoid looking where his collar separated, inexplicably certain that the sight of his vein pulsing *there* would leave me undone—make me press my tongue to trace the pale blue line etched against his skin. Still, to my horror, I said, "You smell good."

Jason raised my chin until I met his eyes. I could feel his gaze track the blush that began from the nape of my neck.

"Amazing, how pink you get," he said softly, as if to himself. Then he immediately circled me until I felt him standing behind me as we both looked out toward where Empress Mindy continued to hold court.

"What do you think of the show?" he asked, the heat beginning to simmer in the sliver of air that separated our bodies.

"Mirrors," I said, struggling for something intelligent to say. "An attempt for depersonalization. No gestures. But you failed . . . only that 'failure,' if you will, is what makes the works succeed. You're painting spaces for the viewer to fill with whatever emotion they wish."

"What else?" he asked. I had to fight not to press back against him.

I gambled and mumbled, "'Overwhelming is the generation's decline,/ At this hour the eyes of him who gazes/ Fill with the gold of his stars . . . .// Softly yellowed moons roll/ Over the fever sheets of the young man,/ Before silence of winter comes'."

"Ah, you understand my yellow," he replied. I thought, but was unsure, that I felt him lightly kiss the back of my head. "I also love George Trakl's poems. Thank you."

I shivered as he recognized the poet I quoted. And I felt that moment to be when I fell in love with Jason Yardley. Panicked, without saying another word, I began to walk away, towards the grey mist of the gallery's smoked glass doors.

But he followed me. I aborted my exit when I heard his

voice whisper "Please." He continued to walk, stepping around me so that we faced each other. His voice was a song as he asked, "Mindy and a few collectors are forcing me to dinner afterwards. Will you join us?"

I sighed as I replied, "Did you think there was a possibility I'd say 'No'?"

As I heard myself, I realized I also caught a hint of what sounded like resentment. That surprised me as much as it surprised him.

He looked at me, his smile fading. He said, "Don't ever hate me. I couldn't stand that."

~~

To support myself, I worked as a packer for the Metropolitan Museum of Art. Over time, the staff had come to depend on me for packing ancient Roman glass.

The other packers, mostly other struggling artists, usually came to work in a fog that scared off the curators of the museum's extensive glass collection. I knew, however, that their daze were induced by works-in-progress which kept them in their thrall. I frequently defended them to the museum's staff, honoring the artists' bemusement with the constraints of reality.

I also wondered why I was so able, psychologically, to leave behind my own works once I shut the door to my studio. Why couldn't I be haunted by my paintings? I once asked my best friend Sheila whether she thought I had less commitment to my art than my obsessive co-workers. I didn't actually think so but had just spent a month of feeling like everything I painted was dreck.

"Naaahhhh. Perhaps you just feel them in a different way—that it so hurts to be separated from your paintings that you can't think of them when you're not with them," she soothed.

"Do you do that?" I replied. "Do you stop thinking of your words when you have to temp?"

Sheila was a poet whose day jobs consisted of temporary typing assignments at Manhattan's huge law firms. As we'd gotten into a habit of doing so once a week, we were eating mustard-smothered hot dogs for lunch on the granite steps of the museum. She took her time chewing before swallowing. Then she looked at me from the side of her eyes and said, "Naaahhhh."

I pretended to swat her with my bag. Then we began to laugh for no particular reason at all since I certainly was not happy then with my progress as a painter. But we continued to laugh. And laugh. It seemed the only thing to do against what Sheila and I understood to be the futility of desiring certainty in the making of art. We laughed so hard that the tourists surrounding us began to laugh, too.

Still, even deep within our laughter, I remained unnerved by being able to avoid thinking of my paintings outside my studio, a bedroom that comprised half of my apartment in Brooklyn. I laughed around a pinprick of pain as a question timidly popped its tiny head into my consciousness: "Wouldn't it be glorious to be utterly lost in fog? Nothing to intrude from seeing inward—where perhaps gray is silver, and yellow is gold?"

~~

"My paintings were all icing, without cake," I said to Jason over dinner, ignoring the Witch and the other collectors who were deconstructing the restaurant's wine list. "How did you see that so quickly?"

"But pretty icing. Like no one's ever created," he ducked my question, his gaze like a warm, salty surf lapping at my body. I could almost hear the sound of seagulls as his eyes pushed away the others until the universe was comprised only of me and him caught within the sunbeam of his sight.

I grappled for self-control and replied, "You're not old enough to be kind to me."

I didn't know what I meant but after I said it, it seemed like the perfect thing to say if I wished not to be enthralled by his eyes.

"Hmmmmmm," he said, then recommended the osso bucco. "They prepare it well here. I'm ordering it, too. If you want, I'll give you my marrow."

"Whatever," I whispered, suddenly deflated and wondering what I was doing amidst these men and women who were all perfumed, tanned and bejeweled. Except for Jason who smelled only of a clean, soapy scent as he leaned towards me.

"Don't be sad," he said, his eyes lingering on the small tattoo of a rose peeking out from beneath my left ear.

"Don't be sad. You have wonderful guts."

~~

Later I learned that he had stumbled into the 7th Boulevard Gallery when he was looking for the Seventh Street Gallery. It wasn't the first time that visitors had confused the two galleries. Jason said he had been interested in the other gallery's show of figurative sketches by Jackson Pollock.

"What interest do you have in Pollock's early drawings?"I asked.

"He had this one gesture I recall from art school—something that's been popping up lately into my dreams. It was the way he drew the curve of a woman's breast, as if he could trace that arc forever. I want to evoke that passion with the lines I use to sunder solid blocks of color. If I must sunder, I must get lost in its movement!"

I was silenced by the fervor of his reply, the physical intensity of how he uttered his words. He looked at me then and whispered, "How far have you chased a dream?"

"I don't, or rarely, dream," I said truthfully.

After a few moments of simply looking at me until I bowed my head to hide from his emerald eyes, he said, "I know. I know you don't dream much. Yet you've already concocted such colors as you have . . ."

His voice trailed off as if he was thinking out loud instead of conversing with me. I could sense him shake his head before continuing, "Tell me of the moon in Mojacar, Spain."

I began to shiver. We were having coffee in a diner. We were seated in a booth encased in thick, red plastic. Under the table, our knees touched. All afternoon, my hands had been conscious of his, often inches away. I began to slide out of the booth but he stopped me. His hands finally came to rest on mine.

"Don't," he whispered. "Tell me of the moon in Mojacar, Spain."

I had witnessed Mojacar's moon when I spent a month five years ago at its Fundacion Valparaiso, an artists' colony. I had been glad of the chance to get away from New York's many distractions in order to focus on my work. But I also had been glad to get away from New York whose boundaries contained a man I loved, but who chose not to love me. He was another artist. He accepted my love. Then he married someone else, a psychoanalyst. I didn't even know Adam was seeing another woman until he announced his engagement to Meredith.

"Honey, you need to understand that there is no future for us unless we want to end up together in an asylum," Adam wrote me. He couldn't even break the news of his departure in person. I felt no consolation from noticing how hard his pen had pressed, so that the paper had torn in some places.

His letter continued, "You make me want to forget my choice to live in the world we've inherited. I made this choice before we met. And, I can see so clearly that you are determined to make your own reality. I don't criticize that—perhaps I even envy this idealism of yours. But it's too much of a responsibility for me. Meredith is a woman who will let me survive my choice. You are the woman who would make me live as a rebel. But, Honey, I am so tired."

I told Jason an abbreviated story about my relationship with Adam and how I went to Mojacar to lick my wounds in private. Attempting to show indifference, I noted that I'd heard that Adam gave up sculpture and moved to Idaho to teach art history at Wayne State University. But I apparently said more than I intended as Jason concluded correctly: "You stopped having dreams after Adam left you."

Jason showed no surprise when I hissed at him, "Don't you dare! Don't you dare feel sorry for me!"

Nor did he try to stop me when I crawled out of the booth and swiftly walked away, determined not to stumble until I no longer felt his searching gaze.

~~

I evaded all of his calls until he stopped calling. But after Jason returned to New Mexico, I began to dream again.

Mostly, I dreamt of tall, butter-ridden cakes oozing with layers of sugar-whipped cream, buried under clouds of more whipped cream and topped with cherries sickly-sweet from their immersion in brandy.

Thereafter, I attempted the logical move of painting these desserts on canvas, over-sized surreal cakes that I wished the viewers to walk into, to dive into until they felt awash in its calories, until they felt the comfort of being returned to their mothers' wombs.

"Yuck!!!! Yucky-yuuuuuuuucccccckkkkkk!!!" Larry said about my efforts when he dropped by my studio. For additional emphasis, he added, "Yuck! Yuck! Yuck!"

He continued further, "Ugh! How monstrous! Ugh!"

Larry articulated exactly how I felt about the paintings.

"It's just that I had spent all my money and four months on these monsters," I sighed. "So I just thought I'd get your opinion, one last opinion, before totally trashing them."

"Well, at least I bring you some good news," Larry said after allowing one last look at the three paintings stacked against the walls. Once more, he shuddered then dramatically turned his back on them.

"Good news?"

"Yep. We sold 'La Luna Naranja.' The buyer didn't even ask for a discount and he sent payment immediately. Which is why I come bearing your share of the proceeds," Larry said, reaching for his wallet from which he drew out a check.

"Who's the buyer?" I said, relieved that at least I found an answer to how I'd pay rent that month.

"I don't know. But he's got an accountant since it was that accountant who purchased it on his behalf," he replied blithely. "Who cares? One of your paintings sold! That's something, right?"

I nodded, but whispered, "It was my favorite. It wasn't perfect but I thought it was the best work I'd done yet."

"Look. We all have our down periods. But I've got faith in you. And the accountant said his client would be interested in whatever else you do in the future. So let's get past these cream cakes, shall we?"

I pulled myself up from the slump I'd fallen into against the wall. I always found Larry insufferable when he got into his paternalistic mode which I could sense was forthcoming unless I aborted it right then.

"Too right!" I said determinedly. "Let's get on with Art! Let's get on with Life!"

"Too right!" Larry echoed. He opened the door to Brooklyn, but looked back once more before leaving. "Besides, how can these cakes work when you didn't even paint your favorite? Chocolate cake? Dark, dense, flourless, chocolate cake!"

~~

Chocolate cake. That night, I dreamt of this dessert I loved but haven't touched for what seemed like years. I no longer ate dessert, and have forgotten when I stopped. I woke up from my dream, my heart pounding as I swore I could taste the aftermath from swallowing a bite of dark, dense, flourless, chocolate cake.

Chocolate cake! Of course! I thought. It was still too early for stores—like art supply stores—to be awake and ready for business. So I descended into a corner of my closet until I found what I suddenly felt in the mood for: an old recording by Glenn Gould. As the piano sounds started bringing the day into the apartment, I began to dance. *Of course!* I thought again. *Of course!*

As soon as the art supply store unlocked its doors, I was in and pushing a shopping cart. *The rent be hanged!* I thought as I tossed in wooden boards and cans of black and white paint. Specifically, I looked for Utrecht's non-yellowing white, the only white that doesn't yellow with age, that remains pure over time. I wanted to create works that would freeze time, unlike the moon's cycle. Indeed, the inevitability of the moon's ascent had compelled me to paint "La Luna Naranja." I had wished to immortalize the virgin moon's flaming beauty through oil on canvas. I paused when I caught my reflection in a mirror. She smiled at me as I thought: *You are an idealist!*

I knew I was imagining it but I could hear Glenn Gould's rendition of Bach's "Italian Concerto/III" spilling out from the store's stereo system. When the piece ended in my mind, I stood still for a moment, paying homage to the composer who so loved his music that he became a recluse in his early 30s to devote his life to it. Then I went home to my studio.

My black-and-white paintings borne that day were showcased during my last show at 7th Boulevard Gallery. Over two years had passed since my other show dominated by "La Luna Naranja." I still missed that painting so much that I was hoping to sell enough of my new works to offer to buy back my painting of Mojacar's orange moon.

I didn't think I could paint anything similar to "La Luna Naranja" again. With hindsight, I realized that it was a painting made possible only in the period of transition which began with Adam's departure and ended with my series of black-and-white paintings.

Comprised of a series of jagged vertical lines against a white background, my latest works signified a radical departure for me. The lines were as dark as my favorite dessert and laid closely to each other so that the white background only rarely peeped through. The paintings were all sized at 20" X 20"—a scale that allowed me more intimacy than did my previous pieces. They were painted on board instead of canvas—specifically board which I'd first laid with gesso and then rigorously smoothened. After painting the surface white, I laid the board vertically against a wall. Using thin brushes dipped into black paint, I then dripped black paint from the top edge and allowed gravity to control how paint would flow down and create the linear pattern. Sheila said the paintings' parallel stripes reminded her of ancient Chinese scrolls of poems whose text she couldn't read but whose Chinese characters she found visually affecting.

The paintings signified another departure as, during the year that I painted them, I couldn't block them from my mind. I so breathed, ate and felt them throughout my days that I was fired by the Met after breaking one of their rarer specimens of antique glass.

Not only was I not surprised when Jason Yardley showed up at my opening but I was delighted. I knew he had arrived when I felt the room temperature heat up, as if the sun had entered the 7th Boulevard Gallery. Of course, it was only Jason's eyes. His eyes grabbed me as soon as he walked through the door. But before coming to me, he first walked along the walls looking closely at each painting.

Then he walked up to me and said, "Doesn't it feel great?"

"Yes," I said simply. And we stood there for a long time, just smiling at each other until others noticed the strange tableau we began to present. But we just kept smiling at each other until others started smiling, too. Then, began by Sheila and Larry, the others started chuckling and then laughing. And we started laughing, too.

After that show, I left the 7th Boulevard Gallery for a prestigious gallery on 57th Street. My last show received critical acclaim even though I and the others at my gallery didn't have any connections with critics or editors of art magazines. Word just spread and the critics, then collectors, attended. *ART EXPOSED*'s reviewer called my works "a cool yet lyrical evocation of transformation, a handsome manifestation of engaging with art history so that the viewer is moved to become intimate with what nevertheless is a rather austere surface." I was heartened as I felt I finally achieved my goal of manifesting what I long held to be as good a definition of a successful painting as I could ever articulate: that organic combination of what engages visual, emotional and intellectual faculties. (I think this is what *ART EXPOSED*'s reviewer also meant, but I'm never sure I fully understand what critics mean.)

With the black-and-white paintings, I and the 7th Boulevard Gallery experienced our first sold-out show. The Witch offered representation, but I opted for the George Adams Gallery because I trusted George. I considered him a person and dealer with much integrity.

~~

I've also left New York to join Jason in New Mexico. In fact, we are preparing for our wedding next month. He insists—and I believe—that he would have proposed marriage even if I hadn't become pregnant with what we hope to be the first of many children. Today, we are installing a crib in the room that will become a nursery. Hanging on its wall is "La Luna Naranja." We agree that it belongs in the nursery—a room that pays homage to transition and then birth.

We realize we have no control over our children's fates. But, to the best of our abilities, we plan to teach them courage—to have the guts to dream. In "La Luna Naranja," Jason says he saw the period in which he was scared of new dreams after achieving immense success—that period when, he now admits, he kept replicating his successful works, scared to dream anew because there was no guarantee that new directions would offer him similar success. In fact, the Witch since has replaced him with a younger artist to highlight as MB Inc.'s star, even though Jason continues to be represented there. But Jason genuinely loves his latest works and that suffices for us to define his success.

Meanwhile, as I adjusted my diet to my pregnancy, I've rediscovered desserts. Dark, dense, flourless, chocolate cake is still my favorite. But, facilitated by the temptations at the French Bakery in downtown Santa Fe, I also now eat leche flan, pumpkin pie, strawberry tarts, lemon mousse and even vanilla cream cakes. How much there is in life to relish!

I've discovered something else in New Mexico—the light. A light that begins each moon with an orange glow. In my dreams, however, the moon is lustrous amber because the colors in my dreams always transcend reality. In my dreams, grey becomes silver and yellow becomes gold.

Jason puts it another way: in dreams, the "silence of winter" never arrives. For silence has no color.

The Caustic Surface

Nowadays, I mostly recall that she once was a hermit, and that she believed that period contained the only happy days of her life. Because she divulged these bits of information months into our relationship, she must have intended, too, for me to know that I did not provide a source of happiness. I marvel that I lingered.

I was hanging three small paintings in a group show at DIS!, a small but prestigious gallery whose artists were renowned for their resonant presentations of color. Self-conscious over the company I was in, as well as that it was my first show, I was torturing myself over whether to line up the paintings laterally, vertically or not line them up at all. The problem in configuration was that one painting was a perfect square, while the other two were differently-sized rectangles. Moreover, one had a protruding surface built up from four months of layering paint to approximate the floor of a dense forest while the others were flatly-surfaced and barely washed with their colors.

"That's the seventh time that you tried that arrangement," she said and, inexplicably, despite the generously heated interior of the gallery, I shivered.

I remember noting the huskiness in her voice before I turned to see Jill for the first time. Her hair seemed to fall forever, its length like the duration of an operatic high note maintained to avoid inevitable death. Parted in the middle and half-covering each eye, her hair dropped in glossy, black waves to her knees, their tips curling like the mist of water breaking from the crash of a waterfall against the surface of an implacable cliff. Next, I saw her eyes glowing at me. They were like green glass hit by light, alternatively translucent and flecked by gold. Finally, she smiled as if it was an act that did not easily occur, the lift of her lips never totally canceling the shadows staining her eyes.

I would come to learn that her face bore all emotion uneasily because she was always looking at something else besides the target locked in her gaze. She could never concentrate on her physical environment as she also was watching her own observance and, equally significant, others' observances of her. She was like Eadward Muybridge, the pioneering photographer credited with inventing the cinema for using three cameras with trip wires to snap photos of motion at three different angles. To help educate artists, Muybridge photographed models in poses that they otherwise would maintain with difficulty, such as the simple act of a raised knee. But he also photographed unusual subjects and, later, she would say that her favorite among Muybridge's subjects was that of a naked epileptic boy sitting in a chair and struggling to stand.

"You were counting?" I replied, observing the slight furrow on her brow despite her smile.

"Only after I noticed your paintings. I noticed them first," she said, then languidly rolled a shoulder to shift the waterfall behind her. When I saw her left eye totally uncovered, I immediately thought of the hearts of sunflowers rising in a former lover's yard long ago. Our affair occured in Munich, which perhaps was what made me unconsciously lasp into German.

"*Wast is los*?" I asked, surprising myself. I usually didn't care about strangers' opinions.

"Nothing is wrong," she replied as if I had spoken in English. "Your arrangement is exactly how you should hang them. Otherwise, you wouldn't keep reverting to that pattern."

Later, she would tell me I lapsed into German and I still wouldn't recognize its foretelling. I carried the scars of Munich long after I left the city in which I loved someone for ten years; it could have lasted forever if I hadn't been drunk when I drove the car that flung my lover through unforgiving glass. Outwardly unscathed, my scars were etched on my heart until my Muse revealed herself to obliterate them without offering relief. For she stripped me into a blank canvas upon which she intended all the marks to be hers. Her name is Jill, and she first approached me to provide direction in a choice I was about to make—to this day, I marvel at the ease with which patterns begin.

For years before she observed my nerve-wracked preparations at DIS!, I had created my paintings only after reading and responding to lines from Jill's poetry. Art, ultimately, is about emotion and I long had relied on her poems to set the stage for my brush, paint and canvas. Once, she wrote, "The sheer momentum of it all, facing the sun,/ Collects the surrendered skin./ Filaments that never crossed the eyelids'/ Undersides leap about unsorted,/ Lifted by their enormous sleeves./ Only the clenched teeth, or the bitten lips/ Connect the heart to its pulsing, the shaken/ Spaces to their breaths, harmonics of oranges."(1) In response, I painted "Lapiz Lazuli," the work that first attracted the attention of Angela Carter, DIS!'s art director.

"It's marvelous how it makes me think of sunlit days, of hot summer days when you're squinting because you forgot your sunglasses and, perhaps, you're having a barbecue, or picnicking in a park or, better yet, at a car race where you know the air touching the hot metal is visible in waves—but you can't really see anything because of the blinding sun. All you can see and, of course, feel, is heat," she said. Fumbling through her words, she was clearly moved. In turn, with her response, I thought of a definition of "Home" I once stumbled across—that "Home" is not one's street address; with Angela's response, I thought I finally found *Home* in her gallery.

I first saw the blue staining "Lapiz Lazuli" while scuba diving. I remember my awe at the darkness of the blue glimmering from the depths of cracked coral, though I still could see the surface of the sea, pale green from the sun's rays. That blue, distinguishable from ebony only with intent attention, was the type I usually saw when I'd dived so deep I couldn't use color to determine direction. When I painted "Lapiz Lazuli," I thought of the sun and that dark, depthless blue—that both were so pervasive and yet couldn't dilute each other. Afterwards, I conceived of manipulating the natural barbarism of colors to exist side by side without encroaching on each other's fields, and, together, present a space for generating an emotional response from the viewer. The canvas of "Lapiz Lazuli" was stained dark-blue, interrupted only by a tiny half-circle of green in its bottom left corner.

After I failed to sell any of my three pieces, I gave Jill "Lapiz Lazuli" because I thought the painting, as conceptualized by me and understood by Angela, marked our relationship with each other. The moment of making that gift still stands as the highest instance of irony in my life. I had thought "Lapiz Lazuli" to be like a lyric poem and that Jill was her "Other" for whom it was birthed, much as I long had considered myself the lucky recipient of her poems whose trajectories I completed through my paintings.

~~

"Otherwise I wouldn't keep reverting to this pattern?" I echoed Jill's words as I looked back at the wall. The three paintings were hung on a sliding scale, with "Land," my forest glade scene, at the top left corner; "Ember," a canvas of pale orange, in the middle; and "Lapiz Lazuli" on the bottom right corner.

I waved my hands, grasped at air and looked at her. She reached forward and captured my fluttering fingers between her palms.

I was jolted by the coolness of her hands. Releasing me, she commanded as if she had the right, "Come. Join me across the street for cappuccino. You need to focus on something else for a while."

She turned and walked out of the gallery without waiting for a response. As she walked past, a part of the waterfall draped itself over my shoulder and I watched it linger before it loosened me. I turned and followed in its wake.

At her insistence, I sat at our table while she took care of ordering and bringing the refreshments. Her cappucino was hot. But she ordered mine iced.

At my questioning glance, she replied, "You looked thirsty. I thought you might prefer something immediately rather than wait for something to cool."

I suddenly felt feverish and leaned a cheek briefly against my glass. Then I sipped it greedily, seeking to quench the sudden parchness in my throat.

"It's good, yes?" she spoke to me like I was a child.

I nodded, still sipping through the straw and looking at her across the rim of my glass. She laughed. It sounded like a windchime, surprising me by its contrast against her low, husky speaking voice.

"There. Don't you feel better now," she said after I leaned back from my first, long sip. Then she pushed forward the gold plate with biscotti sprinkled lightly with confectioner's sugar. I felt like a child as I nibbled on the hardened biscuits. I felt her gaze on my lips as I tasted orange, then mint.

There. Don't you feel better now. She said that on other occasions. She said she liked saying those words to me. Especially when, afterwards, I would nestle my face between her shoulder blades, relish the drape of her hair and circle one hand to hold her cool, full breasts. I would come to discover that all of my memories of Jill are physical: they never fail to evoke jasmine in the air. A jasmine perfume consistently pervaded her hair that flowed like silk against my skin.

There. "There" was one of her favorite words. When she returned to the gallery that evening for the group show's opening, she found me huddling behind a column that hid me from the crowd. She smiled and said, "*There*. There you are."

Then she took my hand and tugged me behind her to the wall featuring my paintings. Still holding my hand, she looked at them for a long, long time while I, beneath lowered lashes, looked furtively at the strange faces surrounding us, some of them looking quizzically at where we stood. They were stunning—the crowd: the right clothes, draped just so over slim, elegant limbs; expensive shoes; exotic perfumes; impeccably-made up faces. I thought them all enthralling. And I was chilled by the notion that they would not be as entranced with my works as I was by them. I heard three cameras click their trip wires and recalled another artist who had found himself in a crowd of beautiful faces, a sight that he felt would have allowed him to birth a new school of painting had he been a painter. Instead, a poet, he wrote, "They feel as close as/ a lunar eclipse outside my window./ I reach out a hand. It passes/

through them. They are made of light./ The curtains billow and the world/ I touch is made of light."(2)

She brought me back to the present when she placed her lips near my ears. I could feel her breath like a warm, undulating sea breeze as she whispered, "Look there!"

She commanded so exultantly that I looked then at my paintings. And I saw that what I created were precious gems, sapphires in three colors twinkling within the boxes of their frames. I lifted my chin and looked at them proudly, as if they were my children playing carrots in a kindergarten play. Then I looked into Jill's eyes and we smiled, then laughed. *There.*

~~

I long have memorized Jill—all of her physical attributes and from all angles. My vision of her remains fractured as, to this day, she remains the one image I am unable to see as a unified whole. To be in her company meant putting on the same three-camera focus on whatever I saw. But while the three-camera perspective diluted her attention span on the physical and moved her back further to her interior world, it only heightened my vision of the visible. Once, I believed this difference to be part of the difference between a poet and a visual artist. I was mistaken. I forgot Malraux's dictum for the young artist: be inspired by a picture of sunset, not sunset itself. I forgot that Whistler was born in the Hermitage and Renoir in the Louvre. I forgot why Picasso noted the logic of Velasquez risking the move to paint an impression and not the actual image of King Philip IV. For a long time, I forgot to become the artist that would meld fractured angles into a vision of unity that would flow then from my hands to the brush to the canvas.

~~

I invited Jill back to my studio after the opening. She said her husband's flight into New York was delayed and had not made other plans for the evening. I remember holding the door open for her and noticing the flutter of her hair once more as she passed me. I recall noting with immense satisfaction that her hair was flowing over the threshold to where I spent my happiest moments. Later, I would read one of her old poems and pause at the lines, "my flag/ unfurls/ a few strands/ sticking/ to your lips."(3) Though written before we met, I would imagine she had been thinking of me. At some point, this would fail to provide consolation.

She paused in front of the work, still only half-formed, on my easel. Then she noticed the xeroxed poem taped by its side. She read out loud, "Sweep the formation/ in the framework of its devices/ there will be no remains/ no signs of pressure/ surprise is real/ the belief that blood circulates/ consolidation occurs in the response." (4)

She raised an eyebrow and I replied, "I love her poetry."

"I'm glad," she said after a brief silence. "I'm J.K. Lang."

She smiled as I froze. She walked over to a bookcase and saw all of her books. She reached for one, turned it over in her hands and began flipping over the pages.

"My," she said, her hands touching the paint splotches on the pages. "They are well used, indeed."

"I'm sorry . . . ."

"No, no. Don't apologize," she said. "I like the fact that they are well-handled, well-used. Is not that the greatest compliment?"

She turned back to my bookshelf, her eyes caressing each of her ten books. They were the only books on the shelf.

"No art books?"

"I don't need them to paint," I said, fidgeting, not knowing what to do with my body as I watched her reach forward once more and touch each one as if she was providing them with individual blessings.

"What do you need my poetry for?" she said, turning back to face me and loosening her cape. The soft dark wool fell around her. She stepped forward as if she was stepping out of something else, something with silk or lace or both. She moved as if she was naked and my hands began to rise, as if to urge her forward.

I continued raising them to take off my coat. Turning away from the slight lift on the corners of her lips that told me she had marked my desire, I said, "Would you like some tea?"

While I heated the water, she returned to the easel and

looked at the painting awaiting my return. It was an abstract piece with thick bands of color curving next to each other. In the kitchenette, over the half wall that separated it from the rest of the studio, I watched her take several paces backward, still keeping her eyes on the painting. After she stopped, she kept looking. From the corner of my eyes, I watched the stillness of her observance. The only thing that moved was her eyes, how they kept flicking all over and around the painting.

"Interesting. Not a single color overlaps over another," she said as I brought her a cup of tea.

"Yes, that's part of what I'm trying to do. Trying to create a unity of colors without the colors edging into the space of other colors," I said.

She smiled at me, "Like a color wheel?"

Later, her slaps would become familiar—I would fail to notice all of them as they occurred in individual incidents. Pain became seamless.

"No. More to symbolize a unity due to a lack of invasion over others' territories," I said determinedly, but self-conscious over my words. I sipped my tea for succor but it scalded the tip of my tongue and I retreated.

"Invasion? Hmmmm. Who has invaded you that you think so low of it?" she said, still smiling as if it would soften her blows.

Mute, I only could look at her.

"Nina, Nina," she put down her cup and came over to me. She placed her palms, warmed by the teacup, around my face.

"Forgive me. I couldn't help testing you."

"Test?" I formed the word as if it was a taste I didn't wish to experience.

"I think your painting is wonderful. You have something there," she said, avoiding my question. Then she slowly moved forward and licked my lips. She drew back then as if to release me. But when I moved forward, she stopped and waited for me. I licked her back. Then she parted her lips.

~~

I named the painting on the easel after her: "J.K. #1." Before I told her to leave so that, once more, I could recognize the variety of ways in which the sun brightens a day, I first had to endure long enough to paint "J.K. #63." And even after she left, I still had to paint through "J.K. #99" before I felt certain I never again would forget how to paint the image of light.

"J.K. #1" was still abstract, still colorful. But the thick bands of colors had been replaced by lines of color. They undulated against a pearly-white background.

"I think this direction, more minimal, is more evocative, don't you think?" Jill said approvingly after I completed the painting. I had implemented the changes after hours of conversation over black coffee, then wine, then black coffee once more.

I replied uncertainly, "It's more poetic?"

She laughed. I felt three cameras click but I laughed back.

She persuaded her husband to rent an apartment in New York City after he agreed to let her build a major contemporary art collection to outfit their houses in Chicago, Telluride, Miami and Napa Valley. I accompanied her to museums and galleries as well as artist's studios in downtown Manhattan, Hoboken, Jersey City, Brooklyn and Washington Heights. She mostly loved the Chinese landscapes at the Metropolitan Museum of Art.

"See there? There?" she would say, lifting her chin towards the paintings of solitary fishermen, hills, waterfalls and bamboo stalks. "See the marvelous relationships between expanses of space and perfectly placed, simple details? There?"

And I would say, *Yes, yes*, though I kept my eyes on her profile, lingering on her parted lips before dropping my gaze down towards the pulse beating on her neck, and then lower to the fullness of her breasts. Sometimes, she would turn her head slowly as if she knew what I was thinking. Amused, she only would say, "There?"

Sometimes, though never frequently enough for me, she would allow me to lead her back to my studio, allow me to take off her cape and fling it impatiently to the side, then slowly unbutton her flowing, velvet shirts until she stood before me bare-breasted, her legs encased in tight black leggings ending in high-heeled boots. She would hold my head against her breasts, saying *There. There.* I loved to cup her breasts, feel their soft heaviness against my palms. Sometimes, I could restrain myself for a few moments and only hold her breasts, lift them up and forward as if I was trying to memorize the pattern of faint blue veins throbbing beneath her pale skin. Then, once more, my tongue would leap and my lips would be locked around one, then the other, then back to the other again. And she would just stand there, her hands on her waist, smiling faintly at me as I would feel her look at me from three angles. Once more, she would say, *There*. Then she would order me to do everything else that would happen that night. And I would obey.

~~

"It's not what I expected," Angela said when she first saw "J.K. #1." I didn't listen to her then.

She sighed and reached for a pack of cigarettes left behind by one of her assistants. "J.K. #1" stood atop a ledge against the wall. The other nine paintings, "J.K." numbers two to ten, were still in their brown paper covers. Avoiding Angela's face, I looked at "J.K. #1." In its lines, I could see Jill's hair floating through air; I could taste their tips, wetting them into strands that would cling against my flesh.

"I thought I quit these three months, two weeks and six days ago," Angela said as she drew out a cigarette.

But I knew she meant something else and walked out of the gallery. I hired a neighbor to pick up the paintings and return them to me. I noticed that Angela looked at the other nine canvases after I left; they were returned with their paper covers creased. Nevertheless, she merely gave them to my neighbor and returned them without a note, without a word.

~~

"She's destroying you," Bruce said. After "J.K. #4," I telephoned Bruce, my best friend, and asked him to visit. It was also the day after Jill and I first made love. Seated on my bed, I was conscious of her presence permeating the sheets. When I revealed that my Muse had become my lover, Bruce repeated, "She's destroying you."

Bruce had saved me once before. I met him after my German lover died. He was my lover's distant cousin who happened to be in Munich during the funeral. Because he didn't know my lover intimately, he couldn't grieve and, from his dispassionate eyes, saw what no other mourner noticed: I had floated beyond my body, not to watch myself as an onlooker interested in what next I would do, but as a cruel stepmother bemoaning the incredible, stunning stupidity that made me sit behind the driver's seat of a car—the sheer stupidity of that move with which I decimated normality. When Bruce returned to New York, he took me with him; my dead lover's relatives had made it clear I would not be missed.

A renowned composer, Bruce frequently traveled. The last time we saw each other, I hadn't yet met Jill. After learning of her existence, he walked over towards my easel. He looked at the beginnings of "J.K. #5" on the easel. He frowned, then walked over to the first four "J.K." paintings against the wall. His fingers left streaks through his damp hair as he impatiently pushed them back from his forehead. His brown hair was darkened by melted snow, matching his eyes which emotion consistently turned jet black. I had memorized how his brown eyes became like non-reflecting black glass since he first turned his stare on me on hearing how his cousin died. They had darkened with pity as he watched me flagellate myself.

"She's destroying you," he said again. A lock of hair fell over his brow as he scowled. "You know better than to paint like this."

He didn't wait for a reply and read out loud from a fragment of one of Jill's poems taped against the easel: "It is almost as if we were there,/ in the shadows and midbar the weather/ devising its human contralto,/ combing the ancient roofs under which we/ the sleepers dream of untrue existences,/ silent as ether, devoid of senses."(5)

"Listen," he said urgently as he came to where I sat immobilized on my bed. He knelt before me as if he was the supplicant. "These paintings don't sing. It's an outrage, how you use those colors meant to evoke light when the surface of the lines are too dense to float. They lie back heavily against the canvas, like spent whips fallen on the floor. They've lost their lyricism—surely you can see that!"

I raised a hand and placed my fingers against his lips to silence him.

"Her poems are lyrical," I whispered.

He held my hand back from his lips and said, "Yes, I agree her poems are lyrical. Perhaps that's what makes what she's doing more . . . more insidious."

I tried to take back my hand but he wouldn't let go.

"I like those paintings!" I insisted faintly.

"They're flat. They're dead," Bruce said once more.

We stared at each other. Then we kept looking into each other's eyes silently. I began to hear the slow drip of a faucet, the faint screech of tires on the streets, a creak on the floorboards overhead, a bird stumble against the windowpane and the weight of our breathing. I heard three cameras click as I saw his eyes.

"We said we'd never do this," he said, even as he unfolded my hands and laid his lips on my lifelines, those creases in my palms that, once, an itinerant gypsy in Germany said were the longest she had ever seen—news that only heightened the despair that had pushed me to seek my fortune from a stranger's lips.

"But did we ever say we didn't want to?" I whispered. He knew then that I was begging.

It was not the cauterizing that I was looking for. I rushed him. Afterwards, I recall thinking as I felt his weight that, in that loss of control, he revealed for the first time the depths of what must have been a long-held desire for me. I rushed him. He tried to be as gentle as he could, but I remained dry and when he no longer could contain himself, the ripping was endless and my wounds bled even more. Afterwards, the morning arrived with rain misting the windows so that the dimness didn't lift with the beginning of a new day.

~~

Jill—or her husband—was generous. She paid the bills for as long as we stayed together. I don't recall how it first began, how I became a "kept woman." She loved to call me that, too.

Once, after "J.K. #15," I asked her why she never acquired any of my paintings for her collection. I was leaning over her, my hands supporting me as I felt her teeth on my breasts. I felt her lips become still before she raised her eyes. Then she slowly fell back against the bed. Her lips were swollen and her translucent eyes darkened into the unreflecting skin of jade.

"My dear Nina," she said softly as I felt her hands descend below my waist. "But those paintings are already acquired. They belong only here, my kept woman, here where you both paint and make love to me. There. Don't you see?"

Then she rolled me over on my back and I was distracted by the underside of her breasts, darker than the cleavage she liked to reveal to the world. That night, she couldn't stay. I returned to where the sheets were still damp and redolent in her scent.

Jasmine. But I remained unable to sleep and returned to my easel. There, I began "J.K. #16," two half circles of white in the middle of a canvas. The bottom half of the vertical, rectangular background was painted black. The upper half of the background was simply canvas, devoid of anything from my brush, from my hands, yet mirroring my heart after I freely emptied it to give her anything and everything.

~~

She conceded she hated her husband.

"But it's not anything I can do something about," she said, drawing her eyes away from "J.K. #27" which we began together after another visit to the Met. Inspired by the paintings of Wang Wei and Li Ti, Jill wanted to see if I could create the feeling of vastness between my lines of color—similar to the Chinese masters' handling of negative space, the voids between objects in their works. By the seventeenth "J.K." painting, my style had become pared down. Each line of color was still layered, but there were less individual lines and those lines had become longer. I also had lost my concern about overlapping colors as the lines now looped through and with each other.

"Why not?" I said.

The shutters narrowed in her eyes, and I could feel her distraction. Dusk streamed through the windows, but I didn't move to turn on the lights. She paced restlessly from one painting to another against the wall, but, I sensed, gave them the barest of her attention.

I asked again, "Why can't you leave your husband?"

"Oh, please," finally she spoke. "Does it matter? I live in an interior world. That's hardly unusual with artists."

Then she looked over, almost slyly at me and said, "Don't you, Nina? Don't you live in an interior world?"

I turned back to the painting but said, "I live where you are."

She didn't cross the chasm that I felt was between us. She didn't cross that negative space to where I stood aching for her to hold me. She only laughed like a wind chime.

Then she said, "Oh, Nina. You don't know what you do to me."

I pressed her again before she left the following morning—I didn't sleep that night, mulling over the possibility of her leaving her husband for me: joyous one moment, then despairing that she would not take the step, then joyous again at the possibility. Daylight was harsh, exposing all of the corners of my studio that recedes as evening approaches. The light was like her voice as she poured herself a third cup of black coffee.

"One can't live without poetry and one can't live on poetry," she said dismissively.

Cruelly, she added, "And sometimes, one can't live on painting, either, my dear kept woman. There. Don't you see?"

I recall this instant as inextricably linked with her cruelty, but the truth is that I was unsure then whether she was being cruel. Before she spoke, I felt the shutters fall over her eyes and I thought she was looking at herself, not me. And she said something else that didn't make sense at the time, that made her bite her lips as she showed that she believed she erred in revealing that thought. She said, "You know, there's at least a five-year time lag between the work I do and the poems that become published."

Before I could ask another question, there was a flurry of leave-taking. Did she have all of her shopping bags from the day before, did she leave anything behind, did she leave behind the presents she bought for me, did I need anything before she would next see me, did I like her brand new wool cape, did I like her old one that she was leaving for me and did I, most assuredly, still love her?

~~

The circle continued to turn. I continued to face a mirror to begin each day. In the immediate aftermath of what I knew to be the beginning of her permanent absence, the departure that I forced myself to precipitate, I could stand in front of the bathroom mirror for hours, willing her to appear behind me, to feel the hair lifted from my nape and see her lips appear in the corner of the mirror and then concurrently see and feel her kiss the exposed skin of my neck, right there on the vein she once said she loved to make tremble. Then it became difficult to meet my eyes.

Painstakingly, each morning, I would look at my pale lips open, allow the toothbrush to penetrate, watch the foam emerge, then sip water from glass. I tried not to lift my eyes higher than my lips. Once, I forced a newly-bought Max Factor Cranberry on them, as if that would make them smile. I never tried that again. When the lipstick rolled off the counter, I let it drop. It still remains in a dark corner today, hidden behind a pipe.

~~

I was covered in orange paint. "J.K. #33" waited impatiently behind me. Jill thought it might be interesting to see what would happen if I tried to use the orange color she first saw in "Ember" in what she had begun to call my "linear series."

"I noticed you've avoided orange," she said unexpectedly one day. Seconds earlier, we were discussing where to eat dinner.

"It's not deliberate. I just haven't found it again in the art store where I buy my supplies," I responded truthfully.

"Really? Then try another art store," she said half-jokingly, as if she didn't believe me. "Logistics should never constrain the creative process, my dear."

And so I began "J.K. #33," eager to show Jill that I wasn't holding back anything from our relationship, even the color orange. But I was struggling. Jill liked my lines dense. But the orange stubbornly remained light, no matter how many layers I piled onto the lines. I thought of widening the lines, but thought that would be cheating. Jill said she loved my lines precisely because they were both thin and dense. The combination, she once said, made her think of the concept of "stickiness."

"Stickiness," she said, a lamp hitting her eyes directly, its brightness almost canceling their green tint. "Stickiness, as in even a fragment of memory, an itch—something unfinished and unformed but which remains inexplicably fraught with meaning, to the extent of being an irritation."

"You think my lines are 'unformed'," I replied, immediately latching onto the implied criticism.

"Not unformed aesthetically, dear Nina," she said, cocking her head. "Unformed as in still in formation and one wonders what the final outcome will be."

After a few moments of silence as I didn't know how to respond, she smiled and added, "But that's good, don't you see? Because the 'stickiness' of your lines, if you will, compel the viewer, not just to observe that you are posing a question but to wish to know desperately what the answer is. That's the appropriate irritation underlying your *unformed* lines."

~~

The orange continued to be uncooperative. When the door bell rang unexpectedly, I felt my shoulders slump in relief.

The first thing I noticed when I opened the door was that he had lost weight.

"I couldn't stay away," Bruce said.

A vein pulsed more prominently than I'd ever noticed around his neck, bared despite the winter chill.

"You shouldn't walk around without a scarf," I said, still blocking his entry.

He merely looked at me, then said, "Let me in, Nina."

I began to shake my head. But when he reached forward, as if to brush away the hair covering my eyes, I stepped back and he moved through the opening. I heard him slam the door behind him as I strode towards the easel. He was right behind me, but I felt him slow down and allow the space to widen between us when he saw "J.K. #33." Three cameras clicked to capture the vastness of the void created by his steps slowing their chase.

I had picked up my brush but couldn't continue. I began to see myself, fidgeting while he looked at the canvas. I saw myself stiffen as he walked towards me and took the brush away. I saw myself begin to speak angrily before he simply laid a finger on my lips. I saw how tears began to fall from my eyes.

I saw how he flinched as the tears wet his fingers, how he picked me up and took me towards the bed, how he held me with one hand while he stripped the bed as he muttered he didn't want to lie on the same sheets she, *SHE*, had used, how he laid me on the bare mattress, how he laid on top of me without bothering to take off his coat, how his hands reached for the bare flesh under my shift as he kissed me all over my face, my neck and through the thin fabric covering my breasts, how he made me arch against him helplessly, how he then tossed aside my shirt and bared my breasts, how he suckled them lovingly—and how my tears began to end.

Then I was back in my body so I could feel more of him. I reached around him and pushed off his coat. Impatiently, he interrupted a kiss to pull off his sweater and the thin t-shirt beneath. And so we laid like that for a while, our hands roaming each other's bare flesh, our lips on each other's. And when he began to lower his face, I felt myself melt at just the graze of his unshaven chin against the hollow of my belly. Then I opened my eyes as I wished again to see. And he held me, guided me, as I felt water surround me and drown me into a deep, deep sleep.

~~

"Bruce," I said his name as if it was a delicacy I wished to taste. He also had fallen asleep. But when I raised my face from his chest, he woke and his arms tightened in the most natural of reflexes.

"We should have done this a long time ago," he said, raising me higher and nuzzling my breasts.

"Bruce," I said once more. But he silenced me.

"We have some unfinished business," he whispered, then grinned as I felt myself blush.

~~

"So, what's the point?"

Beyond the window, the sun was setting. I thought of pointing out the orange streak in the sky that birthed "Ember" seemingly another lifetime ago. I turned to look at Bruce. Fresh from a shower, he was barefoot and his hair damp. He held a beer in one hand as he looked at "J.K. #33."

"I've just begun it," I said.

He turned to look at me and replied, "You know that's not what I mean."

"It's the concept of stickiness," I began, slowly then rushing my words as I continued. "Stickiness, as in, perhaps a fragment of memory, an itch—something unfinished and unformed but which remains inexplicably fraught with meaning, to the extent of being an irritation. A stickiness because the lines are deliberately unformed—that is, unformed as in still in formation, leaving the viewer wondering what the final outcome will be. Because the 'stickiness' of the lines, if you will, compel the viewer to not just observe that I am posing a question and the viewer is 'irritated' into wishing desperately what the answer is to the question posed by the lines."

I felt myself leave my body again. I saw myself drop my head as my babble trailed off. I saw him come over to raise my chin and insist, "Look at me."

I watched myself open my eyes and receive his kiss on my forehead.

I returned to my body to feel him hold me, to feel his heart beating against my cheek.

"Once, you asked me how I compose music," he whispered. "I think I replied with just three words: 'music seems inevitable.' Do you remember how you responded?"

I raised my head to look at him. I leaned forward to kiss him but he held me back and repeated, "Do you remember?"

"I said, 'That's exactly how I paint. The image is inevitable'."(6)

Then he received my kiss. Then he said I still had things to resolve. Then he left. But first he said he would wait for my confirmation that I had overcame everything I needed to resolve. He repeated once more: he would wait.

~~

I didn't know how to begin again with Jill. I still desired her—how could I not, when she had been, still was, my Muse. I didn't consider a new relationship to require a rejection of what we had, just a change in direction, a shift in perspective. But I didn't know how to begin again, and it was this uncertainty, this coincidental rationale, that made me ask to see some of her recent poems. I remember hearing three cameras click in the distance and a strange expression briefly ripple across her face. I remember recognizing it as fear but that I couldn't name it immediately because I had never seen her face form fear before.

"What? Have you run through all ten of my books for inspiration?" she laughed, her self-assured self once more.

I heard the three cameras click again and watched myself reply, "Is that a 'no'?"

"Nonsense, of course not. I'd be delighted to show you some of the poems I'm working on," she said blithely, for a moment making me wonder whether I had imagined her first reaction.

She showed me several pieces. They all possessed the same sensibility as her prose poem, "Ex Ore Suo," which she translated from Latin as "From Its Own Mouth."

> *A cry in the night, in a far distance, though never again to be repeated, can evoke an emotional response. It is understandable in an unstable society that the impetus of much functioning is generated by reaction. Progress requires movement; movement produces noise. Natural sciences monopolized European eighteenth century, an age of poetic sterility. The Chinese say: notice an object by depicting the wind its form interrupts. Spontaneity requires concentration. It should not be confused with a loose tongue. Architects contradict each other as they renovate the same house over time, but they never conclude it is useless to build a house. The theory sprouts from the soil of error. Error is never condemned by a judge, only ex ore suo, from its own mouth.*

The barbarian is defined by his poverty of mythological experience, particularly the learned barbarian who smartly bows to the merits of conception but is "vicious through science."(7)

The interesting thing about receiving her poems is that she said she would wait to hear from me after I read them. And that if, after I read her poems, I didn't call, then she would assume that I didn't wish to see her again. I tried to laugh away this notion as I received the sheafs of paper containing her latest poetry.

She didn't smile as she waited for my laughter to end. She just waited, then said, "Read and see."

After reading her poems, I painted 20 paintings in the "J.K." series—from #34 to #53. Beginning with "J.K. #34," I stopped painting the whips that Bruce saw. But my colors still stained each other. And in every canvas, a lime accent intruded, like the skin of tart, green apples, or the depthless translucence of her eyes.

The green nagged at me, and I thought I must be reluctant to let her go. I called her, and the delight in her voice touched me. I invited her over, with a fleeting thought that nothing need come of her visit. She brought champagne and fat, seedless grapes with the thickest and most violet skins I have ever seen. She said, when she presented her gifts, *There.*

Yes, we made love that night. It was inevitable as soon as she walked over the threshold, her hair flowing as languorously as I recalled. Yes, afterwards, I smelled the jasmine as I buried my face between her shoulder blades, covered by her hair, my hands cupping her cool, full breasts. Yes, she said, *There. Don't you feel better now.* And her hair flowed like silk against my skin.

When I painted the next painting "J.K. #54," the colors separated into their fields. But green wouldn't leave my palette. And the green didn't belong, forcing my hand to cover it with another color.

But once more, I asked her to come over. And, yes, it was inevitable as soon as she walked over the threshold, her hair flowing as languorously as I recalled. Yes, afterwards, I smelled the jasmine as I buried my face between her shoulder blades, covered by her hair, my hands cupping her cool, full breasts. Yes, she said, *There. Don't you feel better now.* And her hair flowed like silk against my skin.

And I kept asking her to come over, even as the subsequent paintings through to "J.K. #65" became a single color, an homage to a memory of sunlit days. The lines Jill loved had melted from their dense thinness, deliquesced to flat swathes of colors. But since she showed me her poems, Jill never again discussed my paintings. I could only hear three cameras click every time she checked my progress on my paintings. Always, she smiled. But she never said a word, never made another suggestion.

The season had changed. I didn't notice until she pointed this out, until she said, "Summer has arrived. What difference, I wonder, will it make?"

Shortly after that, in a gesture out of context from our

conversation, she cocked her head at me and said, "Nina, you surprise me."

Then she was out the door as she returned to her generous husband who was taking her to Sydney that evening to continue her art acquisitions. I walked over to the window to watch her hail a taxi. Before she entered, she turned to meet my gaze and waved. I lifted a hand but she had turned her back to enter the cab. I returned to "J.K. #73" and noticed its dense, multilayered surface. It was a bold red color vibrating in intensity. Not a sign of the tail of a whip.

~~

Insidious. It took me through to "J.K. #83" to realize that Jill no longer had to engage me in discussions over aesthetics. I had thrown off her influence on my art: my colors no longer needed to invade each other. But I still asked, begged, her to visit me. When I realized this, the whip reappeared in "J.K. #84." And continued to appear through to "J.K. #92."

~~

"J.K. #93" was still a blank, pristine, untouched canvas. I had stared at it for three hours, the sweat soaking through my thin t-shirt. I didn't have the energy to walk to the other side of the studio and turn on the air conditioning. I don't remember how long the doorbell rang before I heard it. It felt like hours before I reached the door.

"You look like shit," he said as soon as I opened the door.

"And you've lost weight," he added, tilting up my chin.

"Oh, Bruce," I whispered, before a blessed darkness descended.

Once, I woke to feel myself drink hot chicken soup, then cold orange juice. Once, I woke to feel his lips. When I woke again, it was a new day.

Bruce was sleeping in the armchair by my bed. I stood and tiptoed towards the bathroom. There, I lashed myself with scalding water for a long, long time.

He began to stir just as I returned to him. When he woke, he didn't say a word, just looked at me trailing wet footprints on the floor. I felt myself leave my body and saw my footsteps falter until I stood just in front of him. I saw myself say, "I'm glad you came."

I saw him say, "Should I be glad I came?"

I saw myself fidget, then whisper, "I thought you were going to wait until you heard from me."

I saw him say, "I haven't yet returned. I just wanted to remind you, I will wait for as long as things take to resolve themselves."

Then I saw him get up and walk towards the door. And I felt myself return to my body to feel the pain of Bruce opening the door, Bruce glancing at me once and then Bruce leaving.

~~

Beginning with "J.K. #93," the next paintings were inevitable in their form, became the images they were meant to be, disregarding Jill's motives or, appropriately, mine. Jill called as soon as she returned from Australia; I remembered watching myself listen to her husky voice coil itself through my telephone's message machine. I recalled watching myself stand there, hovering over the phone for a long time after Jill hung up. After two months of my silence, she returned "Lapiz Lazuli" without an enclosed note, but with a check covering what she knew would be a year's rent on my studio. As I sealed the envelope returning her check, I recalled remembering that Jill had said that she was most touched by Muybridge's photos of the epileptic boy trying to stand. I remembered, too, that the boy had failed—he'd quivered his limbs for only as long as the three cameras paid attention.

I ended the "J.K." series at number 99. To end it at 100, I felt, would be histrionic. From "J.K." numbers 93-99, my brush rejected the guilt I hadn't realized still simmered over my actions on that road in Munich. This was as it should be. Art can be therapeutic, but is not therapy itself. As an artist, I wished to attempt transcendence through color—a transcendence over even the realities of the world I inherited but frequently do not understand. I had realized this with the first three canvases that I hung in DIS!, only to become lost as I became part of what I now know to be a mere experiment by Jill to recover her own Muse. Jill replaced the spirit of the cruel stepmother watching me flagellate myself over Munich. She *became* the cruel stepmother wielding the whip I thought I deserved to feel. Ironically, Jill hadn't known the lesson she was teaching me: the Muse punishes for insincerity. The image is not the painter. The image is the image, just as a poem can only be defined as a poem: *without meaning, simply being.*

Later, I gave "Lapiz Lazuli" to Angela, thinking that it found with her the home it deserved. I gave it to her during the opening of my second show. I had renamed numbers 93-99 from the "J.K." series as, respectively: "Saffron," "Celadon," "Lake," "Rose Petal," "Night Lamp," "Summer" and "Burn." All, I felt, were more appropriate for the paintings in which, Angela said, I successfully "manipulated color to attain its own autonomy." Angela captured in words what I long had identified as merely a feeling simmering deep within my belly as I wielded my brush.

"You know, Kandinsky saw the painting's surface as a field where he could create images and find an order more or less independent with his involvement of the picture's surface. But he also said that color could not exist by itself—that it needed a discernible form," Angela spouted enthusiastically as she moved from one canvas to another like a child not knowing with which new Christmas toy to play.

"But even as he placed limitations on both form and color, he speculated that artists one day might manipulate color so that it could attain its own autonomy."

Here, Angela paused to hug me as if she couldn't help

herself. Then she flung out her arms and crowed, "You've done it! Kandinsky would be nodding in his grave—you are what he wondered would be possible, and what the Abstract Expressionists began!"

Then she laughed.

"Listen. I'm giddy. Forgive the melodrama," she said, beginning to hiccup. But she repeated once more, "You are the realization of Kandinsky's hope."

Then she laughed again, and I started to laugh, too, as her joy became infectious. We began to dance around my paintings, like sapphires as they reflected the rays of the sun hovering benignly over the window.

~~

I stopped following Jill's career after reading an interview where she announced her retirement as a poet. She rationalized her retirement by saying she had struggled for nearly eight years to rediscover her Muse, tried "all sorts of experiments" to lure back her presence. A year had passed since she returned "Lapiz Lazuli."

She claimed to reconcile herself to her Muse's permanent departure.

"Besides," she said to the interviewer, "I've decided on my next career, to open an art gallery in Santa Fe where I'm building a new home. This way, I'll continue to be near the wonderful creative minds of artists."

"Anyway," she added, "I can hardly become a hermit just because I find I can no longer write poetry, can I?"

The interviewer reported that she laughed after she presented the question.

The article featured a photo of her standing in front of a cliff. She stood near the cliff's edge as the immediate background behind her was of a vast empty space before the face of a mountain began in the distance. She had cut her hair and didn't look full-frontal at the camera. She had inclined her face so that the viewer saw only what she was looking at as well as her profile, but with no clear idea of how she was responding to what she saw.

A black and white photo, it failed, too, to confirm whether her eyes were still like green glass facing light. And I observed my compulsion to affirm the translucence of her eyes, even as I watched myself and gently mocked my weakness.

Once, I thought of getting rid of her poetry books. But a page fell open to one of my favorite lines: "Because it's not possible to absorb more than one insight at a time, there seems to be a contradiction between the visual or space, and the context or meaning."(8) I thought I could live with her old poetry books, because it was my choice to make and I chose to do so. Besides, I've determined that one can have more than one Muse. I'm looking at art books again—especially those featuring the works of Henri Matisse. Perhaps this century's greatest colorist, Matisse affirms my respect for the flat surface in order to achieve greater compositional freedom. In his paintings, color cannot be separated from the image.

Today, I can trade stares with my reflections. I cry less often, have even begun to smile back. As Bruce told me, there is no need to fear the caustic surface, that surface to which all light rays emanating from a single point and reflected by a curved surface, such as a concave mirror, are tangent. Laterally, vertically, or not lined up at all—the image is inevitable, if the artist only allows for its visibility. With the belief in control as manifested by intention, rationalizations intrude, preventing the surfacing of what should have been inevitable. Transcendence, too, can mean overcoming autobiography. As an artist, I use the darkness I feel still simmering in me to enhance the image, rather than invade it and get in its way.

The "Other"

I hunted Helene because she was his wife and I was in love with him. That's the story of my life: a series of compromises. What mostly surprises me now is how, in the beginning, I thought I would have fun.

As always, Helene was looking at him adoringly. He was expounding, no doubt, on the "parallel universes" for which his sculptures of thick steel squares ostensibly provided "doorways" to experiences which the "discerning" could enjoy—I'd heard this all before as he becomes even more garrulous than usual during postcoital bliss. His show at the Contemporary Museum of Art in SoHo featured the thresholds to 12 different worlds of such experiences.

I looked at him and Helene over the rim of my wine glass from the other side of the wide room. They seemed to gather all the radiance emanating from the halogen lights and bouncing from the white walls as dark shapes contracted and expanded around them from the adoring crowd. He was dressed in Armani. She was also in black, but I mostly noticed the tightness of her clothes which further highlighted her high breasts and narrow waist. I began by envying her figure, then I began to salivate.

She was five years younger than him, a year older than me. She was also an artist and mostly painted small abstract works. She was beginning to develop a reputation, but it seemed likely that it may never be known if any success she will muster would have occurred had she not married the sculptor once heralded as "The Only Artist Who Could Out-Macho Richard Serra." As with most things, it often takes more than talent to attain recognition. Looking at her then, however, I knew she didn't marry him for advancing her career, which was rumored about his first wife. I recognized that light that glimmered in her eyes whenever she looked at him—how, even when she was talking with someone else, her eyes kept shifting until she could locate him within the perimeter of her vision. I still look at him that way. *I will always look at him that way.*

But I couldn't have him. He had been willing to have me as his secret mistress. Once, he had said as he stroked between my thighs while I stood naked before him, "Seurat had a secret lover for years. But her role as his mistress became known only after he died."

I wasn't listening then, or listening as well as I try to do nowadays: I replied by asking him not to marry Helene, thereby breaking the rules of our engagement. He then said it was "the end," which didn't stop him from fucking me one last time. Which didn't stop me from falling to my knees and opening my mouth for him one last time. But, as I often have consoled myself, I was, after all, in love. *I am still in love.*

He hadn't seen me yet, or if he had he wasn't showing any consciousness of my presence. I knew they had just returned from their honeymoon in Capri. They both looked tan. I leaned back against the wall as I felt jealousy rear up at an image of them on the beach, she undoubtedly topless while he smoothed oil on her breasts. I remembered how his hands had grasped my breasts, kneading them from behind silk. I always wore silk tops for him. He had loved to pinch my nipples, then move me around with his fingers still clamped on my nipples. I thought of doing that to her, too.

"I like my sex rough," he had warned me shortly after the first time I had convulsed around his tongue.

"Whatever you want," I had replied and only leaned closer towards him.

A few moments later, I had asked him if I gave him something he couldn't get from anyone else. We both had known we were discussing Helene, innocent Helene, as he said, "Yes."

"Then why. . ." I had tried to ask, but he had silenced me by tightening his hold on my breasts.

"There are certain things we must never discuss. One of them is Helene."

As he had taught me, I whispered, "Yes, Master: whatever you want."

I looked at Helene's jutting breasts and wondered if, just as she unknowingly was unable to satisfy him, there was some need he didn't know about her and, thus, was unable to fulfill. Once more, I considered how so many couples compromise for the end result of being buried in coffins laid side by side.

~~

"I see that you like breaking the square," I said as I circled the walls of her studio. This was the third time I'd met Helene after her husband's museum show. I had introduced myself to her while she was replenishing her wine glass, and managed to engage her in a discussion about her work. Naturally, I had become familiar with her paintings through various group exhibitions in town—I wanted to know anything that even remotely touched his life. Helene seemed to be in a period of featuring incomplete squares within her paintings. The ruptured squares were set against lushly painted surfaces etched here and there with slanting horizontal lines.

"Yes, well. There's no such thing as perfection, is there?" she replied, handing me a glass of champagne.

"Champagne?" I smiled.

"Well, it's your first time in my studio," she said as we lightly touched our glasses together.

Her studio was tiny but had a large window that framed the World Trade Center.

"Oh, those," she replied, almost surprised, after I mentioned the twin towers. "I rarely focus on the buildings. I usually look at the water."

She went over to a file cabinet, pulled out the top drawer and motioned me over to look. I joined her and saw that the top drawer was full of drawings, all evoking waves.

"Hmmm. So the etched lines on your paintings are actually just minimalized portraits of broken surfaces? Like the tips of waves when they swell to sunder the watery surface? How did you come to have such an affinity for broken surfaces, for imperfection?"

"Most people don't see that, even after they see my drawings," she replied, smiling, though she dodged my questions.

I wanted to press her but suddenly noticed how she seemed to be nervous. She seemed to have stopped breathing.

~~

"It's not that I'm not receptive," I said as I finally moved, raised my hand to stop her from taking off her blouse. I had decided to let the silent expand between us, simply looking back into her sad eyes until she raised her hands and started slowly unbuttoning her blouse. But though I stopped her from letting the blouse fall, they already had revealed the breasts that had so tantalized me during his show and which I furtively relished with my eyes at every opportunity.

"I want to please you," she blurted. Then she reached for my right hand and pressed it against her left breast. *The weight of a soft pear: I felt the doves on the windowsill begin to weep.* Silently, I began to roll her pink nipple gently between my fingers as, with my other hand, I raised the champagne glass to the pink nub. She parted her lips when I dribbled champagne on her breast but didn't utter a sound. *I was an eagle: my lips swooped down.*

~~

"Why?"

Of course, I asked her the question only afterwards. Is not such the manner of those who intend to seduce—first physically overcome the target and reserve any discussion for the "afterwards"? I had learned this from him. I stood over her drinking directly from the champagne bottle as she remained in the position I'd left her, lolling back against the folds of raw canvas I had flung across the floor before pushing her down.

As I had done after the first time with her husband, she felt a shyness surface. She began to close the thighs I had parted as wide as she could muster before I left her on the floor. I stopped her when I whispered, "Sssshhh." Then I whispered again, "Spread."

She was my own painting, my version of Courbet's "The Origin Of the World." But her hair was silkier than the coarse, bushy hair Courbet painted on his model. At the moment, the hairs were also matted together from our sweat, which only served to heighten the mouth of the cave still rearing at me, offering at its center a ridge replete from my fingers' furious dance.

"How pink it is," I said, then dribbled champagne on it.

She wriggled, and I loved it.

I asked again, "Why?"

~~

I refused to leave my reflection. I kept staring into my eyes as I considered her replies to my question. Beyond my bathroom door, the apartment whose address I'd used for 20 years felt alien to me. When Helene had said that she suspected he was having an affair, I had only encouraged her to continue talking. When she had said she wanted a woman's love because her experience seemed to prove the impossibility of obtaining love from a man, I had begun straightening my clothes to leave.

Immediately, she had leapt from the floor and flung her arms around me. It was the first time I had noticed her lips nude, lipstick long licked or bitten away.

"Please. Please tell me you'll return."

The best I could do, even as my hands began fondling her breasts then twisting her nipples the way he had loved to do to me, was to repeat something he also once said to me, "I will never ignore you."

~~

I already anticipated the ending of this story. Helene would leave him for me. And I would cherish her and remain faithful to her for as long as she would choose to remain with me. Then, after she left me, I would return to him; knowing we share the same compulsion, he would take me back. But I would accept the risk that Helene might wish to remain forever with me—blocking from me and him a happy ending that we both once revealed to each other to be something we have never known.

I would accept the risk that would obviate a happy ending for him and me for I have only ever been moved by one thing besides him: the story of George Seurat's mistress who was his lover until she died. She even bore him a child. But no one knew of her existence until after Seurat died. Her name is more relevant than the name of Helene's husband, the target of my obsession, for the purpose of this story.

And I recall too as I begin to prepare to trade the unfolding of this text for the unfolding of another reality which includes Helene's voice now singing into my phone message machine, things are often only what they are named. Thus, for the purpose of this story, you may assume that my name may as well be the same two words that comprised the name of Seurat's secret lover: *Madeleine Knobloch*.

It ended badly. I am also surprised to be pained by the knowledge that she is picking and, most assuredly, will keep picking at her memories of our affair. I know she will pick at them over and over like other scars I once caused and which healing she deferred in an attempt to make them permanent against her flesh: she often encouraged my fingers to press deeper by saying she wanted my "marks never to fade." She was pleased to wear my brand.

~~

I only hope that as she painstakingly goes over and over her memories—no doubt vacillating between despair, guilt, anger and a most unrelenting, unrelenting sadness—she remembers to bring the proper significance to my wedding night: the night after I married Victoria despite her pleas that I choose her. She went to an island resort that weekend as, she had whispered wetly in my ear (her breasts so soft, so soft against the calluses on my palms), she did not want that Sunday morning to be in the same city as it hosted my marriage to another woman. She returned late Sunday night, my wedding night. That midnight, I e-mailed her "Hello." One word. Surely, I keep hoping today, she would realize it is significant that I found the rip in time during my wedding night to sneak off to the computer, turn it on, and e-mail her that brief word. Something significant that, should she choose, she can cherish to prove that our relationship meant something to me. Our affair ended badly—now I wonder how long I must try to soothe her in my mind for it is impossible now to soothe her in person, as I once relished every week in a hotel room booked under a fictional name.

~~

She often needed to be soothed, a filly who believed every path she walked was the edge to some chasm so deep one can't see its bottom. Once, she asked whether I found her inexperience "tedious." I recall replying—sincerely—I found her inexperience "thrilling." Now that the affair is over, I realize how inexperienced I'd become with inexperience. This is one difference between her and me: she said, "I love you" and I never did.

~~

I recall the first time I asked a mirror: What kind of a man are you? When I began my affair with her, I was three weeks away from watching Victoria walk down the aisle in a strapless white gown edged with thin lavender silk. Did I think of her—the woman who had to leave the country for the hour during which I tried to lose myself in Victoria's teary but adoring gaze? Surely, when I recited the vows Victoria and I wrote together—when I stumbled over my words as I recited my part of our mutual pledge to be nonjudgmental with each other's "idiosyncrasies" (a word that we had chosen because we knew it would make our friends laugh)—surely, I thought of her? Only hours later would I bring her back to me, a newly-married man, by e-mailing her with a mere "Hello."

~~

The last time we resuscitated our affair, I had warned her I liked rough sex, that I would keep her only as my slave, that I would see her only when it was convenient for me, that I might choose to see her for only one minute with her mouth—and I said all this as one tear seeped from beneath the closed lid of her right eye, a thin vein crackling blue across the pale skin bereft of eye shadow. I said all this as my fingers twisted her nipples. To all this, she gasped, "Whatever you want." Surely I didn't see pain sheathing her face with a generously-crimson glow? Surely, I saw bliss? Surely I thought I saw bliss? Am I cruel?

~~

Whatever I wanted. She often offered that phrase to me. I always enjoyed it, especially when she would expand it to, "Without knowing what it means, whatever you want." I will always treasure one of my favorite lessons of teaching her what that phrase meant. Once, she complained with a pout, her childish manner tightening my scrotum, that she didn't like it when, during our prior meeting, I had replaced her cunt with her mouth. I stroked her hair gently as I whispered back, "But your desires shouldn't matter if you're my slave." I stopped her then with a firmly-planted hand on her back when she would have reared away from my words, watched her face intently as the significance of my words moistened her eyes. I was proud of her when she dammed her tears and choked out, "Yes, Master."

~~

I am surprised that I also pick at my memories of her, specifically my rare sightings of her prior to that first meeting when we began to realize that a common compulsion (familiar to me but thoroughly unknown to her) bound us together. Once, before I recognized this compulsion and named it with her name, I was about to go into a subway car as she was leaving it. I thought about not entering, waiting for the next train. I thought about elongating the nods of recognition we shared from having sufficient mutual friends that we'd seen each other in a handful of large social gatherings. She was dressed in black pants and a black shirt as she stepped out onto the subway platform. I recall thinking that she looked like a line that had just walked off a minimalist Brice Marden print. I felt an unfamiliar sense of my dishevelment—my untrimmed, uncombed hair and shirt missing buttons and flapping over my jeans. But I ignored the unexpected pull toward her and stepped into the subway car. I had had a premonition, I now understand, as I had failed to act on my thought to linger a while with her, only to be surprised at my subsequent disappointment over doors shutting between us: the keenness of this disappointment.

~~

Perhaps one of my favorite recollections was when she first wore a dress to visit me. It was hot outside, or so she said as she entered my apartment wearing a yellow outfit with a long skirt. She had e-mailed me earlier that week about stumbling as she jogged in the park. She said she was thinking of me, tripped on a twig—such a tiny twig! she had exclaimed—and fell on her left knee. All week, she picked at her scabs, wanting the scars to be permanent so that her body would bear physical proof of my effect on her. After she sat on the sofa, she asked shyly, "Would you like to see my scars?" I nodded, then watched her lift her long skirt demurely just to where the scars crowned her knee. Marvelously ugly, the scars were mottled like the skin of old frogs. I bent down and kissed her fragile knee, eliciting a surprised but delighted "Ohhh" from her lips. Then I quickly flipped her skirts up to see pale gleaming thighs that I ached to explore. So I did.

~~

She often asked if I thought she was strange. I always replied, No. I think she needed to hear that. Shortly after we began our conversations, our relationship that had begun innocently with a few e-mails—so innocently, I keep remembering with as much awe as I have ever felt over anything—it was clear to me that this was an adult woman just beginning to shove aside certain conventions in which she'd long buried herself. I thought, she must have been hurt badly as a child that she'd so seek to insulate herself from the world. Later, she would discuss a diaspora that caused her so much pain she decided to become a "rich man's wife." For money, she explained as if I didn't already know, can also provide an escape from having to put one's self at the risk of direct engagement with other people or other factors to which she never wished to cede control. But when she met me, she was beginning to realize the downside of avoiding personal stakes—that is, she was starting to realize risk is essential to experiencing the glory of life. She said she became tired of "merely reading about life's possibilities" in the fictional novels she devoured daily. I didn't point out to her that there's a difference between fiction and reality for I've lived long enough to know there need not be such a dividing line—though such a line is usually healthy. I only nodded, silently recognizing with her statement what caused her to pursue me, a stranger whose bad habits she didn't know.

~~

Once, she admitted, "I had never fallen on my knees before." She admitted it with a relish that I don't think she knew she showed. The pink tip of her pink tongue revealed itself, unconsciously licking the right corner of her lips though it had been several minutes since she had swallowed. Thus, there was a period, Dear Reader, when I thought I finally found someone whom I didn't have to blindfold in order to stop time.

~~

Why did she want me? Why did she cling to me? Why did she have such faith in me? Why did she, in her open-hearted word, "love" me? I was intoxicated with her answers to my questions. She said she long had followed and admired my paintings from afar, ever since I began seven years ago to show at Gallery Winter which was located across the street from her husband's office building. The first time she saw my works, she had arrived 15 minutes early for a luncheon date with the man whose name was the same as the marble building in which he spent his days. She entered the gallery and met "me" then. For she met "me" long before we actually spoke for the first time. Apparently, I had courted her for years through my paintings. This, as I've admitted, was intoxicating. An artist works for so long in the solitude of the studio that it is always nice to hear that the works end up moving someone so profoundly, so affectingly, as she says my works touched her. She bought what was the smallest painting in that show: the 12" by 10" abstract "Circuitous." She said she wanted her first painting by me to be small enough to slide into her lingerie drawer, to become a secret known only to her and covered by the same slivers of silk, satin and lace that had known her more intimately, she says, than any person until I met her. She preferred abstract works, she added, because through her interpretations she could "delude" herself with thinking she still possessed an individual's subjectivity. "Delude"—that word was her choice; I have never seen and see no reason now to dispute her diction.

~~

She often discussed the Milky Way. Up there, she claimed with an utmost fortitude in her belief, is a poker table she dominates. She is, she noted, a consistent winner even though her poker buddies are fallen angels who go through boxes and boxes of cigars rolled on the thighs of Cuban virgins. As long as she can bluff fallen angels, she said with a rare wink, she felt the universe was at balance and that there even was a place for her in it where she never would be judged. You see, she explained while moving seamlessly from fairy tale to autobiography, she long had steered her life based on the astonishment she recalls when her mother picked her up and whispered into her ear, "I am irrelevant and will remain so for the rest of what I know to be a tediously long life, and there is absolutely nothing I can do about it." At the time, her mother was 25 years old and she was two years old. During our last meeting, the last time I saw her, the last time she tasted me and I her, she mentioned that she'd been losing badly at poker—this, I interpreted to mean that her insomnia has not prevented her from experiencing nightmares at night. This is yet another regret I have about our affair—that, as a result of its ending, she no longer wins at poker. I know her victories had provided such pleasure, and how rare it is for her to find pleasure. She also said it wasn't until she started losing that she realized that her angels possessed eyes with no color. I asked what a lack of color looks like. She replied, "Like my father's face will look when he lies on his deathbed. Inexplicably, I anticipate that his face will speak to me with a grief I will begin, from that moment on, to emulate. I anticipate that his face will utter gently, 'May you transcend your mother'." I didn't bother asking why she would wish to emulate her father's anguish, not because I didn't care but because I did care.

~~

This story has always been about her. This story which, I am surprised to discover, has engaged my heart. It engages me still. Before her, I can't recall ever missing something: I have long recognized that emptiness defines me. I can't recall the beginning of the emptiness that defines me. This story is only about her. What does this say about me? For, this time, I am not unscathed. But I do not know what that means. Once, she said that until one learns compassion, one can never experience revelations. This, too, is something I do not understand. But I recall her statement for the record as this story is about her. About her—including: once, shortly after the first time she called me "Master," she said she went to the public library to conduct research. She said she doesn't believe in originality and guessed that books have been written about her. She was right; here is an excerpt from one of the many books about her:

> *From One Submissive's Perspective: "By being submissive, we are slowly tearing down the protective walls built because of some things that happened in childhood. For me, (submission) . . . is a way of confronting my fears and allowing myself to grow emotionally."*
>
> ***—from "The Loving Dominant" by John Warren a.k.a. "Mentor"***

This story has always been about her—is that correct? Once, she said, "You will always be inside me." And I? I feel her in the very air against my cheek. But this story is about her. Still, though the story about me also has been told a million times before, perhaps I should begin to write it, too.

~~

I can make a prude learn to wear red stilettos, learn to lick a shoe so she can move a glistening heel slowly down her body, between her breasts, then slip it into that forest that Courbet once painted and called "The Origin of the World." I can make the strongest learn submission then crave to submit to me over and over again. But time is the greatest betrayer—at the moment of feeling at the height of my powers, she found a rip in my mask, slipped through and taught me that I should not avoid my own "I." It is an "I" who feels powerless when the whip is still, when handcuffs are empty and limp on the floor, when a woman has slipped on the silk blouse to cover the ebony clamps I had placed on her nipples to remind her of my orders for the next time. Who is this man who knows himself only as a mask? Who is this man who can never paint a perfect circle. How did I learn to rupture circles or transform them into ellipses to evoke the act of departures? Why must I keep tracing over and over the arcs of these imperfect circles? Who am I circling and circling as I look for the man whose shadow I have cast over the faces of many women on their knees? Why, for the first time, have I been moved by a slave? Who is this man who, for the first time, is leaving objectivity for subjectivity—who, for the first time, wishes a particular face on the naked body tied to the bedpost?

The Art Collector

At the intersection of hedonism and jealousy you will find the collector. When the collector acquires one of my works, I become objectified—undoubtedly, this is one reason why I prefer my sex rough and that I dominate. For in roaming through the art world I've met most of my collectors. To varying degrees, they believe they own me when they acquire my paintings or sculptures—and I object.

Art, in all of its forms, requires an audience to attain completion. My paintings are both more demanding for and contingent on this relationship. Abstract, sometimes minimalist, they do not spoon-feed images to the viewer. The viewer must be able to look at my paintings and be the one to place on their canvasses whatever is seen, then felt, then joined. The viewer must invest as much as I did in the creation of the work. When I meet collectors who use eyes, not ears, to see, I always hope they fall in love with my work. They are the ones I like to collect.

But until I met her, I never arrived at this intersection of hedonism and jealousy. The pursuit of pleasure, yes. Jealousy, never until her. Until I met her I never wanted any of them so badly I didn't wish anyone else to touch their bodies—to touch them with the eyes, hands, mind and entire length of a body pressed against theirs before physical penetration. Until I met her, I was unable to empathize with Bill Gat who cheerfully spent half his fortune to finance an army of art world denizens searching for a sculpture by Phidias whose gold and ivory statue of Athena embellished the Parthenon. At the time the billionaire began his search, no one knew for certain if such an object existed. But the founder of MicroTech had been obsessed with the possibility since he saw Athena immortalized by this sculptor's hands and after the possibility was raised by a junior professor at the University of Athens.

"It is widely believed, but no one has ever proven, that there is no surviving work by Phidias besides what's at the Parthenon. With your fortune, you might be able to find out the answer to this centuries-old question," noted the enthusiastic academician.

Gat bit. His generous budget beat the odds. With his money, a team led by the young professor who happily took a sabbatical from academia turned up a Phidias figure in the basement of one of the houses owned by a British aristocrat. Fortunately for what had become Gat's consuming passion, the skinny man with pale blue blood inching through his veins needed a significant monetary infusion to keep a stable of leather-clad boys and anorexic girls happy. The underaged fillies weren't the only reasons the aristocrat wished to remain anonymous. The aristocrat understood the significance of the Phidias sculpture lurking in his basement: his ancestors must have stolen, bribed and murdered in order to successfully smuggle the figure out of Greece. Now, Gat seems destined to spend the remaining half of his net worth fending off attempts by the Greek government for the sculpture's return. Yet, in a recent interview published in *ART EXPOSED*, Gat professes no regret and the magazine's cover photo shows his eyes twinkling with glee as one hand smugly fondles the thigh of a now-headless woman. The figure is believed to be from Phidias' first commission when Pericles ordered statues to decorate Athens.

At first I was overjoyed to find myself standing at this intersection to which I hoped my works would bring others—I've envied that twinkle in Gat's eyes. Collecting is about only one thing: possession. And I long wished to know the feeling of being possessed by the thrall of the target.

It is enthrallment that I know is also familiar to Paul Stavris who is currently dominating the art news headlines. Stavris was firmly ensconced in what he anticipated would become his death bed when he announced that he was donating five red figure vases by Exeias, a Greek potter from 530 B.C., to the Greek National Museum. The shipping tycoon—through his public relations lackeys—contextualized the donation as "yet another exercise of Stavris' vaunted nationalism."

Pathetic—sure, acquiring the rare vases probably cost a hundred million dollars or so, but that's nothing to the billionaire. He waited until he was dying to give away the collection—what does that imply about the strength of his political loyalties? Once more, I considered the many ways in which we delude ourselves so that even someone supposedly reliant on seeing must remain blind. *To collect is to possess.*

To collect is to possess, and I also long wished to experience a type of longing so overwhelming I could lose myself in the body of my obsession. Precisely because it had never happened before, I wanted to know how it feels to be felled by desire for a human being. Before I met her, I was able to experience this combination of hope and hunger only when immersed in creating one of my paintings or sculptures, or while writing a poem. But I longed for this soul mate who would allow my engagement with both the risk and thrill of the unknown factor introduced by someone else. I longed to be enmeshed in an insatiable hunger for an "Other."

The "Other"—someone who looks at my works and, by looking at them, breathes life into them. I collect only the collectors among these "Others"—they who have enough money to afford my creations. After entering my collectors' homes to find myself bent over their compliant naked bodies, I like to look up once in a while to see one of my paintings winking at me from a wall or a sculpture applauding from a corner. In such manner can I feel the perfection of a circle: the collector chased my work, then chased me, only to become the caught target when our bodies collide. The collectors—not me or my works—become the ones objectified, their bodies mine to manipulate like the paints on my canvas, or the metal I mold and stone I break to become my sculptures.

Through my acquisitions, I hope to learn how to paint a perfect circle freehand. My only source of self-doubt—that is, until I met her—is over my ability to draw, and I long believed I will be possessed by this doubt until I manage to paint a perfect circle—its pure form. My attempts usually lapsed into ellipses whose bulges remind me of secret desires that long to break free, or circular fragments whose tips seem bereft. But I wish to manifest the pure form of the flawless circle. I do not wish my attempts at purity to depict the banal display of fettered freedom or miserable fragments—I do not believe myself unusual in this regard: I prefer not to be sad.

I laughed when I realized that the "Other" for whom I'd long searched and dreamt is also an artist. "Of course!" I thought to myself again when I saw her own works. At the time, she was painting tiny color field paintings, about 10 X 10 inches each. Then she would embed screws against the fields so that the metal head(s) became the mark(s) against the canvas.

"Positioning is important during penetration," she said quite seriously after I asked her about her work. She was in a group show whose opening I attended because it included a video installation created by a friend's son.

"The positioning influences color as well," she added as I worked on blocking my amusement from showing. "Usually, if a penetration or series of penetrations occurs by the edge of the canvas, the color field will be of light shades, like pastel. If I insert a screw, say, into the center of the canvas, the colors are typically bolder, even garish."

I was charmed. She hadn't yet began to recognize, hence have a shot at articulating meaningfully, her search. That's all right—many artists never grasp art in a way that would allow them to express the visual through language. But I did like her attempts and her seriousness at it. That's when I finally realized what had been missing from the others I collected: the empathy for the creative process. I wondered then about upgrading my collection to focus it only on artist-collectors. But most artists would not be able to afford my works. This only made her more precious to me. She is as rare as a Barnett Newman painting on the market once his wife decided to hoard his paintings and place them only in museum collections. Her rarity exacerbated my jealousy. I wished to be her only possessor—a factor that strengthened my resolve in the immediate days after our first encounter: *I would be her Master*.

She was a virgin when we met. By this, I meant that she did not yet know how to long for the blindfold. It was exhilarating to wait, to dampen my compulsions and behave like an ordinary mortal courting her. That she considered me her "Muse" only heightened the effect of my ministrations, and I took full advantage of the benefits offered by her having mythologized me. I watched her blossom, intrigued, too, by the effect of what I inspired as, in her words, "the Muse looking back." At one point, she reconsidered her colors, learning to mix colors into an ostentatious blend that made me think of heat—as from an unblinking sun pouring into a desert until it cracks the earth. Only one other living artist beside her has evoked the blister through color: Will Tosso, a painter who puts his paintings through months and months of being smeared or layered with paint. His studio is effectively a dungeon for paintings: canvases hang on the wall awaiting his hand. Typically, a painting gets sprayed by the paint that he intended for another work. The canvases sweat and drip for months, sometimes years, before he allows them to leave his studio. Her process is gentler—she lays her canvas flat on a table or the floor, depending on its size, and rarely addresses an area larger than her palm at any point in time. For both artists, however, color is hot—even seemingly radioactive. *Heat is the critical goal*—she once shared while she writhed below me, her sweat pooling on the tile floors of the bathroom. She added, "I've come to detest pastel."

Once, she sent me a thousand-dollar bill with five rose petals in a heavy-weight, cream-colored envelope used by one of New York's most expensive hotels. That I taught her to communicate in this manner only made the correspondence more thrilling. I rewarded her at our next meeting by pushing her down to the floor as soon as I entered the room and locked the door. Room 720 of the Peninsula Hotel, at the corner of 57th Street and Fifth Avenue, in Manhattan, New York.

J. Paul Getty has written, "I am convinced that the true

collector does not acquire objects of art for himself alone... Appreciating the beauty of the object, he is willing and even eager to have others share his pleasure. It is, of course, for this reasons that so many collectors loan their finest pieces to museums or establish museums of their own where the items they have painstakingly collected may be viewed by the general public."

Crap. These are collectors who do not see solely with their eyes, but must also see with their ears—usually, they require the aid of a "consultant" to determine what to hang on their walls. Utter crap. There's more honesty to the Japanese billionaire who acquired a Van Gogh and kept it locked in a private safe whose contents are available only to his gaze. Which is another way of saying I appreciated her value because she is rare—an artist who also used collecting to feed her art because she considered all of her life material for her art: she saw no lines between her studio and the rest of the universe. Her process is circular, not linear—and also synchronistic with the width of her eyes. Once, I teased her about her wide-open gaze; she replied, "My eyes are wide to pull in more of the world." She favored as a slogan: *Maximize Lucidity!* At first, she couldn't help herself from closing her eyes during our early days when she would gasp at things she'd never experienced: the flat of my palm against her buttocks, the belt tying her wrists together, her grandmother's silk scarf blindfolding her eyes, the bite of my teeth on her pink nipples. Her shyness only enhanced her charm as well as made the veins on my dick redden and throb. Then, as I anticipated, she began to keep her eyes wide open to see. Then she began to keep her eyes open to enable me to witness her glistening abjection. You see, I taught her to please me. *Whatever you want*, I taught her to whisper to me.

~~

Agnes Gund describes herself as a collector who keeps her art, even during the 1980s when everyone started to trade the works of certain artists like Jasper Johns and Willem deKooning as if they were stocks on Nasdaq. That the former president of New York's Museum of Modern Art never sold works from her collection partly explains why Jasper Johns himself would visit her to realign the stretchers on his piece. Her Johns painting was valued at about $17 million at the time. But "if you sell it, you don't have it," Agnes Gund says. Exactly. To collect is to *have*.

The Artist Looks At the Model

She was not the wind. Not then. Behind her, molecules formed an empty grey blackboard. She stood as an offended crack intent upon rupturing any seamless plane. It was clear she was oblivious to popularity. Still, I noticed her breasts—they were credible fortitudes.

~~

She could have shed her flesh and it wouldn't have mattered to my measuring palm shaped as an "L." I was surveying bone resigned to an impending break. Most assuredly, an explanation existed. Will I learn it, I wondered, given the speed of her velocity? To a landlord, she might have seemed a salt statue. To me, her red-rimmed eyes denoted the exhausted pace of a replicating light-year.

~~

Suddenly, my feet ached for her femur. But I knew better than to display my flinch—it would make her reach for the steel-tipped whips which I wished to be the one to wield. I pushed back my hair. I instructed saliva to wait.

~~

My fingers swiped at wet clay to rationalize my periscopic sighting of her toes. So much like young toads from an underbrush in Brazil. Such flaws will not prevent me from jogging when she will have learned to quiver like a 19th century theater. She will instruct her thighs to accommodate my brandy.

~~

Another tenant instructed her to shift 45 degrees. She conceded her poverty at spatial relationships to approximate a different angle. We were all moved. In sympathy, one of us pawed at air. I obviated zero gravity: I honed in.

~~

Dear Marigold: Cease using K-mart cream. It is always better to be the mistress. Over the centuries, germs have been neutered to avoid succumbing to silk pavilions embossed with blue dragons. I shall place you on a cushion concocted from the emptying of an emperor's aviaries. Then I shall rush to be cruel as I know you are up to it. Despite your paucity of petals and thinning seasons. Sincerely, An Old Gentleman From The Old School.

~~

That first day, she inspired a cube of clay. "What does that mean?" she queried as she tightened the belt to her rented robe. I answered by truculently shoving air with my chin. It expanded the whites in her eyes. But, as I expected, it also parted her lips. Shyly, but willingly, her green tongue peeked at me.

~~

No one is impervious to Romanticism. Perhaps I would have stayed seated in my oversized corduroy armchair. I had turned professorial after all with a box of Cubans harrummphing by my side. Damn that itch that blocked the pinkness of her wrists.

~~

"Never before," she acknowledged through a set of contexts as varied as my promiscuous judgments on the same slice of weather. Plus, I am a Grand Master at using names to create. Once, I called her a "landlady." I was riveted, watching her try to fix my plumbing. I counted as, one by one, her fingernails betrayed their French manicures.

~~

She became the wind after she lost all misgivings about drying my feet with her hair. It was a day bequeathed by a leap year. She forgot the word she had saved secretly for a special occasion to unload on me—such a big world of meaning in what would have been spelt as a couple of letters: N-O. It would have been. Such a big world.

~~

This time, I used both palms to shape "L"s into a frame. She was the wind, but still too gentle. "You can do it!" I egged her on with sincere irritation on my unshaven face. I molded wind into a body for nothing is risked without bacteria. I felled her to her knees. She was up to it. Once, she jutted out her lower lip. I bit it. She was up to it.

~~

Once, I prevented myself from weakening as she continued to leak. When she first saw rust, I reminded myself, she claimed she throbbed. Thus, my fingers continued to dilate.

~~

She also throbbed from evacuating mornings. How would she look through a window? Would she remain indifferent to the same view of a neighboring building's backside from behind the velvet-draped windows of a hundred hotels? My depicted conclusions of her eyes are unable to transcend bleakness. She is forever a ripe rose.

~~

She is nothing new. Nothing new has frozen since *The Kritios Boy* (circa 590 B.C.). Appropriately, she called me "Absence"—which will only facilitate her blusters at alvinophilia. But. There was a reversal in an alley deeply hidden within the bowels of Gotham City. She called me "Muse." There was an about-turn. There was an about-face.

~~

She longed for conversations—this is the only manner in which she is a girl. Her eyes are wide to pull in more of the world. Others misunderstood and used the nature of her grazing gaze to label her "Innocence." I never believed: she is intimate with cognac and port. With mahogany walls. She is intimate with empty bottles.

~~

I will concede her interior is an effective compass. While she ruptures the blackboard, I am unable to form anything but circles and squares. She demands I invest interpretations on her flesh now poised vs. pósed because she is the wind. I hide in concepts stuck in the theoretical realm. I am surprised to be pained by the scar traversing her belly. White fringes hair. *It is good to feel,* I whisper as a failed partition.

~~

Underwear became artifact. Then concept. I barely cross thresholds before her thumbs are at my belt. *If she was a kitchen,* I gleefully speculate. She has traded in flesh-colored pantyhose for vermilion stockings bruised by black. How now to remedy her complaint that I have never called her "Peony"?

~~

I wanted to catch her on paper. I drew a stage. I tried again, muttering through a sincere fever. I drew a pedestal. There was a reversal in the back seat of a cab cruising through the fake palm trees of Miami: a useless determination. The incentive persists as a lie.

~~

Rain does not forgive. Rain is indifferent to what it wets. I lower *The Wall Street Journal* to peer at her. She is the wind. She is a hurricane seated in my kitchen, stealing my eggs. For, she forgot to say "Please." I shall remind her of manners. She is wind, not rain. Presumably, I am rain.

~~

She likes the word "translucent." I prefer the word "transparent." Once more, I am unable to fathom why I prefer to be an envelope versus the perfumed snapshot slipped in. Perhaps to be stamped: DO NOT FOLD. Perhaps.

~~

She is the wind. I profess pleasure at her transition before returning behind-the-scenes to nurse a cognac I will never empty from its crystal goblet. My professed control may or may not compensate for the harsh truth: I continue to possess and be possessed by a limbic brain.

"Blue Richard"

The first time I laid beneath him on his bed, I thought gray paint stained the hollows beneath his eyes. As if I could lick away the shadows, I couldn't help myself from darting out a tongue. But he swiftly captured it with his lips and I drowned. From the far distance of the streets, the sounds of raucous horns and vendors yelling in Chinese only made me grasp him tighter. Once I opened my eyes towards a window and noticed the fall of dusk surrounding a red neon sign flickering.

He took me to Africa. Drums sounded in the distance, far behind the rain that fell outside our tent and served to enhance the warmth of its interior. Or, perhaps I only thought it would be appropriate to have invisible men beating on taught animal skins to provide an arbitrary rhythm for my uncontrolled heaving as he lay before me, willingly pinned beneath my thighs while his hands held my swollen breasts to his suckling lips.

The first time he noticed me, another woman was leaving his lips. He was tall so that she had to reach up to his darkly-tanned face, allowing her also to press her breasts against the white camellia painted across his chest. It was winter in Manhattan, but he wore a short-sleeved Hawaiian shirt.

He caught me staring when he lifted a Bass ale and used the movement to wipe off the pink stains from his lips. I quickly looked away, but not before he managed to lift an eyebrow at me from across the crowded room of the gallery. Beyond the window, a street lamp flickered through the mist. I heard rain end.

Later, he had my back against the wall. He said he liked my paintings that were hanging in the group show. He was the gallery's most important artist. I shook my hair forward to cover my eyes. I peered at him and mumbled, "Thanks. Not like your paintings, of course."

I meant it as a compliment. He pretended to misunderstand and said something about the individual vision unique to each artist. But what I recall most clearly was the graze of his fingers against my cheek as he drew away the curtain of hair that hid my eyes. His fingers were tipped by calluses whose roughness on my skin I wished would never end. Later, he would say he noticed me part my lips at his touch and he had to force himself to walk away.

He called me after we met at the gallery. I looked at the hour as I heard his voice. "5 a.m.?" I asked. "I wanted to wake you," he replied. Then he told me to go back to sleep and dream of him. I dreamt of him using a knife to slice away at the tight rubber pants encasing a redhead whose hair matched the stains on his lips. She also wore a black thong that fell as he flicked a blade. She wanted to lift a cashmere sweater to show her breasts, but he said it wasn't necessary. When I woke, my cheeks and thighs were wet.

He insisted on feeding me dinner that weekend, but I met him unexpectedly on the street the day after I dreamt of him. I was looking at a painting through a window. "The artist failed," his voice rippled through my hair like a breeze. "How?" I asked as he turned me around to face him. "Because in painting a woman dropping an orange, the artist painted the orange in mid-air," he said before placing his lips on my cheek, then lingering there for a while as I stood, immobilized. "A fall is always complete," he added as his lips shifted to touch the corner of mine. Snow began to fall as he walked away.

~~

The sake was cold in entering. "Heating it hides imperfections," he said as he refilled my tiny cup. I raised my cup once more to avoid his eyes, even as I felt my first sip begin to simmer within my rib cage. The clear liquid revealed a series of blue concentric circles on the bottom of the cup. I tasted tart green apples as I took a second sip. I noticed a vein throbbing on his wrist. I could feel his gaze on my lips and wondered what he looked like when he smiled.

After dinner, he took me to a party in a neighborhood I didn't recognize. The party was in a brownstone and its revelers spilled forth onto the sidewalk. He was greeted with happy cries as soon as they turned into its street. We walked towards the sounds. The other houses on the block were dark, with no signs of life. Light sparkling through all of its many windows, the brownstone glimmered like a solitaire nestled in black velvet. I felt his friends' glances like little stabs. He introduced me to no one. He merely circled an arm around me and spoke over my head to the others. They kept coming up to him as if they couldn't help themselves. I found it easier to cling to him and bury my face beneath his chin. The others kept stabbing at me.

He left me once, shortly after midnight. He drew back and breathed against my closed eyes. "Look at me," he whispered. After I obeyed, he said he had to talk to someone in another room. "I'll be right back," he promised. He returned after two hours. I was in the corner of the room where he left me. He saw my eyes grab him as soon as he looked through the doorway. He took his time walking to where I sat trembling on a chair, where I had been ignored or stabbed by the others. One woman in the first hour of his absence hissed, "He'll leave you, too," as she pretended to place an empty glass by the table next to my chair. In the second hour, a man tried to engage my breasts in conversation until I bluntly said, "Go away."

I wouldn't look at him when he finally stood in front of me. I watched his hands slowly lift to reach for me. He drew me up and returned me to the comfort of burying my face beneath his chin. "I wanted you to know what it is like without me," he whispered as he tightened his arms. I could feel his heart beating erratically. I refused to look at him, even when he said, "I'll never lie to you again." I refused to look at him until he added, "I missed you, too."

"No," I said the next day, and the day after. "No," I repeated again when he called the following week. Then a new month began and I marked it by having dinner with another man. Afterwards, we went to listen to jazz at several clubs. I was drunk by the time I also rejected him and left the cab that returned him to where he came from. For a moment, I stood there watching the cab's orange headlights recede. I thought, "He would have been kind." I noticed a slight mist turn its way onto my street. When I turned towards my door, he was waiting for me.

I walked up the stoop and tried to ignore him. But my hands shook as I tried to insert the keys. His voice was soft as he took them from my hand and opened the door. "I'm glad you turned him down." He followed me into the foyer. I made another effort, stopped and said, "I can manage from here." He lifted his hand and palmed my cheek, then began rubbing his thumb against my lips. "No, you can't." I fainted into his arms. When I woke, I was in my bed, naked. It was morning and he was nowhere in sight. I had flung off the bedsheets and the sun was warm as it streamed through the window, melting the ice on its panes.

I rose and walked towards the full-length mirror behind my bedroom door. I saw bloodshot eyes drop to the rest of my body. I noted one breast was still slightly smaller than the other, the bones of my ribcage still protruded, my waist still expanded into my hips, dark strands still curled around each other between my thighs and the birthmark shaped like a tear still stained my left thigh. I also noticed my nipples were puckered as if they were small fists, tightly clenched. I reached for a note stuck in the side of the mirror. He had written, "I love the teardrop on your thigh."

He rarely smiled with his lips. I had to look into his eyes. It took me a while to discover this because I fought him for a long, long time before I first drowned in his arms. The second time was in the bedroom of a stranger hosting a party. The sounds of cocktail chatter and a string quartet permeated through the closed door. I slowly unbuttoned the high neck of a silk dress and let it fall. At his request, I had worn nothing underneath. I walked to where he sat on the bed watching me intently. I sat on his lap and hid my face in the nape of his neck while he stroked my breasts. Then he picked me up and laid me on the bed. "Open your eyes," he whispered. "Keep them open," he added as he parted my thighs. "Keep them open," he whispered again as I began to undulate against his fingers. "There," he said. *There.*

But I did fight for a long time. "No," I said when he called the afternoon after he left me a love letter to face when I sought my reflection. "No," I said again the following day. A few days later, I saw him across the street from my door, leaning against a car and an unlit cigarette within his lips. He had seen me first and watched my steps falter when I noticed him. He continued to watch me walk towards my door, open it and step in. He didn't try to stop me.

I visited the gallery during the last day of the group show which featured two of my paintings. I stood behind a column trying to listen to the comments of an elderly couple who had paused in front of my works. My dealer had whispered they were well-known art collectors. I saw him enter the gallery and divert their attention. "Sweetheart," the wife called out and he walked over to join them. He gave no sign of noticing me, though he must have seen me. "What do you think of this painting?" she asked, touching his sleeve familiarly. “A lot of promise, but not quite there,” he said after giving my painting three seconds. “Dear, that's what I told you,” the man told his wife. “Let's talk about you. Do you have any new pieces?” I heard them make an appointment for dinner before I walked away and out the door.

I paused in front of a red light and felt my heart beating quickly, desperately. “You could join us for dinner,” he said. I wasn't surprised that he followed me. I turned around and looked into his eyes. He was smiling. “Come, let me buy you a black dress,” he said, taking my hand. My rage died and I felt separated from my body, as if I was curious to see what I would do next. He paused before we entered a small, expensive boutique and raised both my hands. He started rubbing them as he observed, “Your hands are cold.”

“Monsieur,” the designer and shopkeeper greeted him familiarly. “It's nice to see you again,” she said as they traded kisses on each both cheeks. I refused to utter a word even when he introduced us. Her smile didn't slip as she asked him, “A black dress?” She turned towards a rack and confidently chose five outfits. Four were mini dresses while one had a long skirt with a thigh-high slit. “Mademoiselle, after you?” she said, drawing aside a curtain to a dressing room. He asked to see me in each outfit, smiling each time and ignoring my ankle-high workboots. Afterwards, he said, “I'll take them all.”

“It's the first time Monsieur has bought more than one outfit at a time,” she whispered to me as she packaged the dresses.

I replied brusquely, "I don't care." She smiled serenely and said, "I don't believe you." When I opened the boxes later that day, I discovered she had included sheer black stockings and a different bottle of perfume with each outfit.

I chose a dress at random and wore it to Chanterelle that evening. By each table, huge mounds of lilies bloomed, their scent weighting the air. I had insisted that I would meet them at the restaurant. "Don't forget or pretend to forget," he whispered after raising my chin with one hand and brushing aside my hair with the other. I kept my eyes closed and said, "I never break my promises." He responded, "Neither do I." I opened my eyes when I felt he wanted to kiss me. But he didn't, only rubbed his thumb once more over my lips.

The art patrons were pleased to meet the young painter who, he said, showed immense promise. They also had bought one of my paintings after I had fled from the gallery. "We agreed it would be a nice way to encourage a promising artist," the man said. "But I genuinely love your painting," his wife quickly added. I spoke only to her after that, carefully ignoring both men. Afterwards, he said, "I'll take you home."

I let him in but, before we could take off our coats, demanded, "How dare you!" He smiled and took off his coat and flung it on the sofa. "Let me," he said, turning me around and taking off my coat which he threw over his. Then he picked me up and carried me into the bedroom. "No," I said. "I know," he replied and laid me gently on the bed. Then he sat beside me and began to watch me. After a few moments, I closed my eyes and whispered, "Please."

The third time I drowned, it was my birthday and he had reserved a suite at the Plaza Hotel. The fire blazed. We sat opposite each other on armchairs encased in gold and red brocade. As he sipped cognac, his eyes never left me. "Thank you," I said about the emerald pendant dangling on a gold chain. "I'd like to see you wearing nothing else." My fingers fumbled as I put it around my neck. Without looking at him, I began to take off my pearl earrings, my silver watch and my jade ring. Then I looked at him as I stood. Slowly, I stepped out of my shoes and rolled down my stockings. His face remained impassive even when I stepped out of the damp fragment of lace that had sought to cover my flesh. Then I drew the dress over my head. I stepped back into my high heels before walking towards him. "You're right," he said as he dribbled the remaining drops of cognac on my breasts. "The emerald and your legs in high heels." Then he licked my breasts as I arched my back, my fingers lost in his hair.

After he took me home from dinner at Chanterelle, I had whispered, "Please." I opened my eyes. "No," he said. "Not yet." Then he leaned over and kissed me on my forehead. I grabbed his arms as he started to withdraw. "Please." Easily, he freed himself then held my hands still against the bed. Still, I raised myself and tried to kiss him. He kept his lips still as I pressed them with mine. "Please. Don't you want me?" I pleaded. Without a word, he withdrew. After I heard the front door close, I wept before dropping off into a fitful sleep. When the phone rang the next morning, I knew the hour was 5 a.m. He told me to dream more dreams and go to his studio in Chinatown that evening.

As I walked into his studio, I saw myself as he sees me. The paint was still wet. "I just finished it," he said. "Until last night, I couldn't finish it." Most of the color were in my eyes, enlarged off scale and with red cracks across their surface. The rest of the painting was in shades of white criss-crossed by thin, black lines. Despite the bloodshot eyes, the figure posed in a relaxed, almost serene manner. Why last night?" I asked, firmly keeping my eyes on the painting. "Look at me," he said. When I met his eyes, he said, "Because you knew to beg."

The first time I laid beneath him on his bed, I thought gray paint stained the hollows beneath his eyes. As if I could lick away the shadows, I couldn't help myself from darting out a tongue. But he swiftly captured it with his lips and I drowned. From the far distance of the streets, the sounds of raucous horns and vendors yelling in Chinese only served to make me grasp him tighter. Once I opened my eyes towards a window and noticed the fall of dusk surrounding a red neon sign flickering.

"Others must have wanted you," I said after the first time, my face buried beneath his chin, his hands slowly rubbing my back. "No one showed as much promise," he said. I raised my head and looked into his eyes. He was smiling. "Promise at what?" He quickly flipped me on my back and started nuzzling my neck before continuing to my breasts while his fingers teased my thighs.

"Promise at what?" I gasped insistently even as my hips pressed towards his fingers. But he wouldn't say and I soon stopped asking, trying instead to breathe.

The last time I drowned, we were surrounded by Africa. Drums sounded in the distance, far behind the rain that fell outside our tent and served to enhance the warmth of its interior. Or, perhaps I only thought it would be appropriate to have invisible men beating on taught animal skins to provide an arbitrary rhythm for my uncontrolled heaving as he lay before me, willingly pinned beneath my thighs while his hands held my swollen breasts to his suckling lips. Thrice, I gasped, "Richard."

The next day, he left early for a safari while I stayed behind to finish a series of paintings for an upcoming show. The next time I saw him, he was barely breathing. The guides had shot the lion, but that was no consolation. "Please," I begged. But he died in my arms. Before he closed his eyes, he smiled one last time.

In New York, my show opened to rave reviews and was quickly sold out. "You certainly lived up to your promise," the art collectors said after they bought two more of my paintings. I finished another glass of wine before asking, "Did Richard ever mention what he first saw in my early works?" She smiled and patted my arm gently. "Oh yes, dear. Richard said, you would have the courage to fall completely. Fall completely—didn't he have such a way with words?" Her husband nodded and said, "These paintings, for instance, you can walk into their center forever. In your early paintings, you hadn't yet figured out, as a critic once said, how to punch that hole in the canvas."

I forced myself to smile, then accepted their congratulations once more before excusing myself. I walked into the gallery owner's office and shut the door behind me. The painting I withdrew from the show was still poised on a chair. I walked towards the canvas with heavily layered brush strokes featuring a vortex that spun into a center of a dark-blue circle. In each curve on the top half of the painting, I saw his eyebrow raised at me. In each curve on the bottom half of the painting, I saw his smile. I followed the curves in "Blue Richard" until they led me to the center where I drowned so that I could feel his arms lift me up to breathe.

Einstein's Love Story

Her face is so clear
that when you gaze
on its perfections

you see your own face
reflected.
—from "White Skin" by Ibn 'Abd Rabbihi
(trans. Cola Franzen & Emilio Garcia Gomez)

She held up the page featuring a review of my sculptures and announced, "Sheer crap!"

I stopped admiring her legs—how they curved yet sliced through the air below her maximized-mini dress. I raised my eyes to look into hers. Jade. With gold-striped irises. Like the heart of sunflowers. Cat eyes.

"Are those corn rows?" I pointed my chin towards her hair, the blonde, skinny braids ending in black, wooden beads floating above the red velvet on her shoulders.

"Wax and steel—distinctly unrelated but harmonized together in sculptures by Einstein," she read, ignoring my question. She paused to look at me over the magazine which halved my view of her face. Cat eyes peered suspiciously.

"That can't be your real name: Einstein," she declared.

"I agree with Erica Jong who suggests that every creative person should choose their own name. She says, select a name—take a name, even if it's the same one with which you were born, as 'an act of faith or an act of intention'."

It never failed before with women: my quoting Erica Jong. Makes them purr like baby lionesses. They don't have to appreciate Erica. It's simply that, as one lady whispered into my ear, there's something intriguing about a six-foot, muscular, bearded sculptor consistently uniformed in Levis over black, steel-tipped, cracked-leather boots quoting the author of "Fear of Flying." In the summer, I replace my denim shirt with a white t-shirt so sheer and tight it paints my chest like a wash of watercolor. Or so another lady said while she laid her cheek on my permanent tan, the t-shirt a puddle of milk by her bed.

"Erica Jong?"

Uh, oh, I thought.

She lowered the magazine to show an elegant but distinctly scornful sneer curling her cranberry, beestung lips. Lucky bees.

"Einstein—a name you chose poorly. If you think you are believable with your lines mined from Erica Jong, then you probably would not fathom why I call this crap. Utter crap!" she snapped, waving the magazine as she backed away.

"Sheer crap," I said as I moved forward with her, as if there was a string between us that pulled me forward one step for each step she moved back. She stopped. I walked forward an extra step, then stopped, too.

"What?"

"Sheer crap. That's what you said. Not, 'utter crap'."

She threw a lightning bolt from her eyes. I refused to be

immolated, bounced it off my denim-clad chest and lifted one eyebrow.

"Seriously—you don't like my work?"

I gestured towards my steel and wax sculptures throughout the gallery, empty of witnesses to our skirmish. Winter had laid a white blanket over SoHo. But even if the weather was more conducive to gallery-hopping, no one seemed to pay much attention to sculpture. It was 2001.

"I didn't say that," she said. Her cat eyes blinked, then looked around me as if searching for the gallery owner. But I knew that Jeff—the owner and my good buddy—was over at the Greek diner getting some coffee. I knew we were alone in the gallery.

Her eyes—cat eyes—returned to mine.

"Actually, I love your sculptures. I think they're brilliant," she said.

I kept looking at her. There were worst ways to spend a Saturday afternoon.

"You called it crap. Sheer crap. Then utter crap," I said, affecting a drawl. My drawls were usually as effective as quoting Erica Jong. This time, it stumbled, then slid, off her corn rows.

"Not the sculptures. Not these," she said, waving towards my babies looking resigned to their loneliness. They were accustomed to waiting for more than a token glance from what little traffic passes them by. "The review. I think the review is crap. Sheer crap. Utter crap!"

After a moment—during which I mentally waltzed her

through the gallery, circling each of my sculptures which had monopolized the most recent six years of my life—we smiled at each other.

I walked towards "Untitled No. 5," a sculpture comprised of two equal boxes: a 16-square-foot block of wax set atop a 16-square-foot block of steel. I turned to face her, the sculpture a comforting presence behind me.

I remembered that review. The critic called my works, among other things, "gay, insouciant compositions out of seemingly unrelated elements. The choice of materials seem coincidental but effectively depicts harmony."

My hands had clenched into fists, hidden from her gaze by the bend of my elbows as I folded my arms.

"What do you mean?" I asked, relieved my voice did not crack.

"Well," she said, as she started to move in a circular path around me and "Untitled No. 5." "You are quoted as saying that your main objective is to 'maximize the very beingness of the materials that you utilize.' You say that you contemplate each material until you understand it completely, a process that you say can take you up to three years for each material. You say that you avoid injecting meaning into your works and that what is important to you are the sensual and visual qualities of the material."

She paused at the farthest right corner of my perspective as I stubbornly continued to stare straight ahead. Then she moved, slipping out of my sight. And I felt immediately alone in an Arctic landscape without horizons until I heard her voice again.

"On the other hand, the critic said your works have a spiritual quality, a sense of yin and yang as you combine unrelated materials into harmonious, unified creations. Nonsense—you don't care about unity and harmony. You juxtapose steel and wax because this combination serves to emphasize the steeliness of steel and waxiness of wax. The two materials starkly contrast in color, texture and density and the contrast separate the two materials in the viewers' minds even as they see them combined into a single sculpture."

Her voice sounded as if she had walked to stand directly behind me. I struggled not to turn around.

"Yin? Yang? Sheer and utter crap. You said exactly what your works are about. The materials. The essence of the materials you choose."

She eased back into the farthest left corner of my sight, then floated until she stood directly in front of me, then stopped and slowly walked closer until she stood directly below my lips. Thankfully, she tilted her face so that I looked into her eyes rather than onto her boney corn rows.

"You're a sculptor. You choose shapes and forms for a reason. For instance, take the piece behind you. A solid square box of wax emphasizes the waxiness of the material. A gigantic puddle of dried wax on the floor wouldn't achieve the same effect, nor would a gigantic candle. People are accustomed to the sight of candles and dried, dripped wax. But a perfect square box of wax—that's unnatural, unexpected. It draws their gazes to the wax, makes them do a mental double-take, triple-take, then makes them question what they're seeing. Among a variety of responses from viewers, all unanimously, at one point of their reaction, observe and note the obvious, 'That's wax!' "

I decided to flirt.

"Why are you so sure there can be no unity, no commonality, between steel and wax?" I asked, losing the drawl. "Take the effect of age: steel sweats rust and wax hardens further into a series of dried slivers. Rust and dried wax—they both flake off at the gentlest touch."

She smiled at me like I was a little boy in bloomers whose tongue had just pushed a scoop of ice cream off its cone.

"That they both flake with age is not a unifying factor. The nature of their aging only serves to focus again on the nature of the materials, the corrosiveness of steel and the brittleness of dried wax—the steeliness of steel and the waxiness of wax," she replied.

I responded with a strong desire to reach forward and ravage her right then and there on the white-stained pine floor of Jeff's empty gallery. Before I could act, she turned and walked away.

She strode to another piece, "Untitled No. 4," a steel pyramid, two feet high from the center of its base to the apex, with a perfectly round ball of wax, four feet in circumference, seemingly poised on the pyramid's tip. (A difficult piece to make.)

"Ultimately, you choose to combine wax and steel together specifically because the two are discordant, yes?"

She smiled at me as she laid her palm gently on top of "Untitled No. 4." Her fingers unconsciously started a caress, as if she was fondling the scalp of a beloved bald man. I felt, though understood it was my imagination, a rush of warm air past my ears. I blinked and saw her clad in a white diaphanous gown that molded itself against her figure, her breasts, as the wind blew at her. Her hair became loosened and flew behind her; her hair became so long that they draped over "Untitled No. 3," "Untitled No. 2," "Untitled No. 1" and "The Very First Untitled" standing patiently behind her, waiting for her next move, silently watchful like bodyguards. I anticipated my face slumbering against the perfumed silk of her hair. I anticipated the scent of white lilies whose thick, waxy folds have always captivated me and made me try to mold the air in my hands as I envisioned how a petal could curl its edges without breaking.

"Because steel and wax do not look comfortable together, you choose to combine them—not in search for the harmony that the critic claims to find in your sculptures. You combine them because they can never be in harmony and, thus, they emphasize the materiality of each other. You maximize for the viewer the essence of the materials, a viewing of steel as steel and wax as wax!"

I heard an exclamation point after each of her declarations, even though she spoke softly. Cat eyes blinked and I felt each eyelash paw at my heart.

"Ultimately, like other masters of abstract imagery," here, she paused briefly, a slight crack appearing on the eggshell smoothness of her pale brow as she seemed to consider whether her passion was causing her to be melodramatic. But she continued, "you cause the viewer to consider—reconsider—the essence of nature, of the universe. The most perceptive will ask that age-old question, 'What is Life?' "

Then she dazzled me with a grin, making me recall the whiteness of sunlight during the aftermath of an unseasonal rain in the midst of spring.

She finished lopping off the heavy burden that had weighed on my shoulders for as long as I had been a sculptor: she concluded, "What a gift you offer: a meditative road towards Enlightenment."

A "master of abstract imagery" offering a "road towards Enlightenment"—I appreciated her pause as to whether all this was just a bit much. I, however, didn't consider her praise overwrought, more like a glass of spring water if I was a black-faced miner stumbling out from the depths of a coal mine. My long-dead sculpture teacher; Jeff; and this lady with blonde corn rows and sheathed in a red mini dress numbered three people who have understood why I decided to spend my life as I have, and as I planned to continue doing: creating sculptures most people will never see and even less will ever understand.

I unfolded my arms. I unclenched my fists. I walked

towards her. When I reached her, I went down on one bended knee and took her right hand in mine. I started hoping desperately that I could lose the macho, womanizing persona I had donned seemingly centuries ago to camouflage my vulnerability to my wax and steel babies. I replied:

"Will You Marry Me?"

Engraving 2

II. FLASH FICTIONS from "ONE"

"ONE" was a bar in Longyearbyen, Norway that closed after its effects included causing too many suicides. For "ONE" was a bar where each patron must drink alone, and Longyearbyen has a law against dying because permafrost prevents bodies from decomposing. These flash fictions were discovered scrawled on paper napkins by one of the workers charged with demolishing the bar. He took them home to his niece, Eileen R. Tabios.

Polmost Spirytus Rektyfikowany Vodka

—after the Temple of Kukulcan, a Mesoamerican step-pyramid in the Chichen Itza archeological site of Yucatan, Mexico

He woke from a dream of Chichen Itza where he'd followed the serpent descending the step pyramid of the Kukulcan temple. When he left its last step, he stumbled out of the dream to feel his cheek hardening against a wood counter. He raised his head to see the bartender looking at him quizzically as she raised a bottle of Polmost Spirytus Rektyfikowany Vodka. "You sure?" the bartender asked, flinging back wavy red hair over gleaming white shoulders bared by a strapless top. The vodka was the world's strongest alcoholic drink, courtesy of Poland. At 192 proof, it was banned from even checked baggage traveling into the United States. He'd excavated it in New Zealand from a wine cellar owned by a Silicon Valley financier who built an escapist utopia on the island country. He'd filed one of the cases in the bar for his private stash. "Not sure. But pour it anyway," he replied. As she filled the glass before him, he asked, "Do you know the word 'seasteading'?" "Nope." "It means creating artificial islands." He'd learned the term after punishing the financier for hiring mercenaries to assassinate a Māori activist concerned about the safety of sea creatures. The bartender snorted. "If folks want to live on islands, they should just come here. The Philippines has 7,641 islands—most are uninhabited." He nodded and tried to recall his dream—he was searching Chichen Itza for a mural depicting the Mayan rain god

Cháak. The mural featured Maya Blue, a color he needed to see to verify he'd successfully recreated the technique for making it. He'd found the dye's source in the Ch'oj plant growing in Quintana Roo. But he'd had to persevere through tests that initially disputed its existence. A cloth soaked in its dye first turned white; only prolonged immersion turned it blue. "I was unnerved by that white smoke until the vibrant turquoise broke through," he explained to the bartender. "No one ever talks about how much fortitude hope requires." The redhead looked at him closely. "But you didn't lose hope," she said. "So what are you doing here?" He looked around. He laughed. He was in "ONE," a bar where each patron must enter alone, drink alone, and leave alone. He laughed again as he waved at her to refill his glass. "A toast to Polmost," he said with a grin. "It made me forget I both lack hope and am hopeless."

One Eye Open

—after coins emblazoned with dolphin-riders in the city of Taras, an ancient Greek city

He sometimes wondered if he should wear an eye-patch to mask how his left eye hid under its constantly lowered eyelid. But he couldn't release dolphins from his memory and chose to be transparent about his shuttered eye. Before retirement, he'd worked for a company that turned dead bodies into ocean reefs—the company named itself "Eternal Reefs." Trawling oceanic depths, he stumbled across a pod of dolphins. He smiled at them, manifesting the long ties between their species. The ancient Greeks and their gods welcomed dolphins—emblazoned on their coins, they were sacred to both Aphrodite and Apollo. In Hindu mythology, the Ganges river dolphin is associated with Ganga, the deity of the Ganges river. The Boto, a species of river dolphin that resides in the Amazon River, are believed to be shapeshifters, or encantados, capable of bearing children with humans. On land, studying them, he stumbled across research revealing how dolphins are sufficiently intelligent to be capable of self-awareness, the precursor to advanced thought processes like meta-cognitive reasoning (thinking about thinking) attributed to humans. Events that blackened sky before nighttime then transpired to interrupt his meditations on dolphins. Those events explained the logic to how dolphins sleep—with one eye open. Those events continued so that he, too, began sleeping with one eye open. Eventually, the only source of succor left to him was "ONE," a bar where patrons must drink alone. He felt relief at being in a place where no one was allowed to bother him. But he'd seen how the affable dolphin sleeps, and so drank his bourbon with one eye open. Paradoxically, one open eye made him more watchful than two open eyes. Blindness, even in one eye, emphasizes one's fragility through exposure to events that randomly create collateral damage, whether from humans who are the planet's most dangerous species or panda cubs smaller than mice and each weighing no more than four ounces. To look at a panda cub is to feel one's heart constrict from the ineffable so that, helplessly, tears begin to leak.

Brutality

—after the Parthenon Marbles

(also known as The Elgin Marbles)

Mr. Doe felt the ghost of Lord Elgin on the empty chair across the table. Britain's Ambassador in Constantinople at the start of the 19th century, had stripped the Parthenon of its most beautiful marbles, over 200 blocks now ensconced in the British Museum. While interest has focused on the stolen marbles, less attention has been paid to how Lord Elgin came to visit the Parthenon: through a royal decree by the Great Vizir authorizing him to do sketches and castings of the Parthenon and its friezes. A century-and-a-half later, the sketches were scheduled to be exhibited at the Bogota Museum of Paper, which was how Mr. Doe came to steal the sketches; he planned to keep them within his private collection until the British returned all Parthenon marbles to Greece.

Mr. Doe hired Laura of Clan 18, one of Bogota's gangs, to hijack the sketches during their transport from the airport to the museum. Laura decided to seduce the manager of its transfer, Gordo. She became his girlfriend some weeks before the scheduled theft. Gordo was exactly what his nickname stated: fat, correction, huge at nearly 7 feet tall and 450 pounds. Such girth, while impressive, made him unpalatable to most ladies in the market for a romantic relationship. Since Laura was a natural beauty and even more charismatic when she shoved her cleavage high through push-up bras, Gordo fell... heavily.

She stroked Gordo's ego by professing awe at his importance for being charged with abducting Lord Elgin's sketches, which was how she convinced Gordo it was his idea to bring her along for the ride. To make a long story short, Laura, an expert in the Soviet martial arts of combat sambo, overcame Gordo and brought their car to a location where three ruthless members of her gang waited. They then scooted off with the sketches they later traded for beaucoo bucks with Mr. Doe. During the hand-off, more to make nervous conversation with the bad-ass-looking gang members than curiosity, Mr. Doe asked, "What happened to Gordo?"

Laura paused, then traded glances with the others. None could hold it in for long: they started laughing, with one actually falling to the ground as he held on to his belly. "How to put this?" Laura began, before succumbing to more laughter. One of the ruthless ones finally explained—'twas easy enough to put several bullets into Gordo's big head. But then they field dressed Gordo as if he was a moose. Yes, a moose. Apparently, they'd trained themselves through YouTube videos of Alaskan hunters field-dressing huge animals. They cut up Gordo's remains and wrapped his meat portions in butcher paper. Later, they offloaded Gordo as beef to a restaurant due to host the engagement party of a rival gang's leader.

Mr. Doe had sold the sketches long ago to another collector. He could not abide the memories that accompanied them—a big man being field-dressed into generous slabs of faux filet mignons.

He roamed the world trying to leave behind his memories; when he accepted the memories will never leave, he found himself in Manila. He thought the premise of "ONE"—enforced loneliness—fit his fate.

But, unbeknownst to the staff of "ONE," a bar where each patron must drink alone, he always has company as he downs shot glasses of the bar's oldest whisky. The whiskey boasts a dark amber color as well as a nose of cinnamon and gingerbread with hints of orange and oak. The palate opens brightly with orange notes before giving way to cinnamon, clove, and gingerbread, followed by a long, spicy finish. Across Mr. Doe's table, Lord Elgin drank as if ghosts were solid and could drink. Lord Elgin even waxed enthusiastically over how the whiskey was made: "It begins with a 100% corn mash bill aged three years in a heavily charred Virginia red wine barrel. The spirit's then transferred into a charred Cinnamon Whiskey barrel where it ages for a year. Then it's transferred again into a used #4 char bourbon barrel where it rests for an additional year, culminating in a one-of-a-kind 5-year-aged whiskey!"

Then Lord Elgin would burp and conclude as he always did with the whisky's name, his wet tongue caressing each syllable: "Bru-tal-i-ty! *Brutality*!"

Sipping at his cruel drink, Mr. Doe would nod in miserable agreement. "Brutality."

Non-Fungible Armadillo Shells

—after "Everydays: the First 5000 Days" by Mike Winkelmann aka Beeple

Soon, the waiters noticed how the man's lips only stopped moving when he sipped from his glass of Reyka vodka. Nearby, the television's Talking Heads debated whether NFTs could work as Pokemon cards, a discussion that involved the bored apes owned by Jimmy Fallon and Paris Hilton as well as how Beeple's NFT collage, "Everydays: The first 5000 Days," sold at Christie's for $69 million, about $15 million more than what Monet's "Nymphéas" sold for in 2014. One waiter approached the muttering man. But the man's muttering was too low for the waiter to hear clearly. So he moved closer to the experienced drunk and observed, "Reyka is a uniquely Icelandic splash in the vodka world. The distiller makes its spirit from a glacier's pure spring water after the water passes through a 4,000-year-old lava field." The man turned his face towards the waiter who took a step back at seeing eyes not just blood-red but with blood leaking from its sides. "TV people are idiots," the man whispered. "I turned a boy into a paraplegic because it's impossible to turn an armadillo into an NFT." Such was how the waiters at "ONE," a bar where each patron must drink alone, came to pity the man with red eyes whose mutterings were simply a repetition of the one word, "idiot." Unlike many on the planet, armadillo shells are bulletproof. Outside the bar, the crumpled receipt for an NFT that failed to shield a boy manifests *flotsam and jetsam* as it keeps being picked up by a harsh wind that blows it down dim and smelly alleys leading nowhere.

Bar-Hopping Sentences

"I hope we'll be best friends when we grow up"—that's what he said to all of them. Turn left and you're on your knees. He woke from a dream of Chichen Itza where he'd followed the serpent descending the step pyramid of the Kukulcan temple. Legendary CIA spy Krii Amman once swayed atop a table in Ye Olde Cheshire Cheese, the London pub known for its regulars Mark Twain, Sir Arthur Conan Doyle, and a foul-mouthed parrot called Polly who spewed profanities and entertained drinkers by imitating a cork popping followed by the glug, glug, glug of wine being poured. He wasn't sleepy but yawned to regulate his body temperature—that was his token health activity. He sometimes wondered if he should wear an eye-patch to mask how his left eye hid under its constantly lowered eyelid. Like the others, he rarely spoke beyond ordering the first fill and subsequent refills—such was the usual state of play at "One," a bar where individual patrons must drink alone. His stomach growled since he refused to do as the Koreans do when they drink their soju. Mr. Doe felt the ghost of Lord Elgin on the empty chair across the table. Soon, the waiters noticed how the man's lips only stopped moving when he sipped from his glass of Reyka vodka. Guilty Pleasure Music wafted from speakers behind the bar. One night, you looked up from your glass of Peacekeeper American Bourbon Whiskey that you'd bought for its bottle shaped like a mobile ICBM missile and, suddenly, all the other patrons felt familiar.

Engraving 3

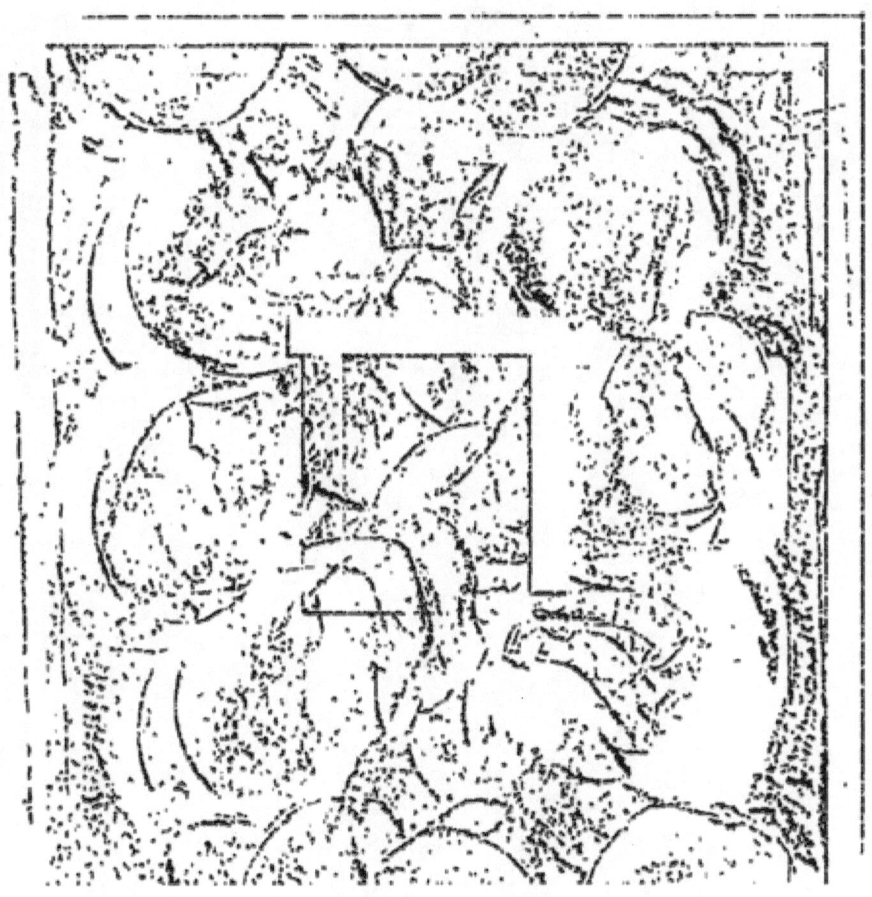

III. THE LEGACY OF LEONARDO DA VINCI'S "VITRUVIAN MAN"

"Leonardo di ser Piero da Vinci[b] (15 April 1452–2 May 1519) was an Italian polymath of the High Renaissance who was active as a painter, draughtsman, engineer, scientist, theorist, sculptor, and architect. While his fame initially rested on his achievements as a painter, he has also become known for his notebooks, in which he made drawings and notes on a variety of subjects, including anatomy, astronomy, botany, cartography, painting, and palaeontology. Leonardo is widely regarded to have been a genius who epitomised the Renaissance humanist ideal, worldview centered on the nature and importance of humanity."
—Wikipedia

Ant-ish Lesson

As a garbage disposal truck, the 2016 Autocar Expeditor Labrie Expert 40/60 split body drives me nuts. I much prefer my MV Pot-Belly Rocket where all trash, regardless of recyclable components, are dumped into a sphere (belly) attached to the rocket that penetrates outer space on its way to the Trash Planet. When that planet is full, earthlings then launch a broklear bomb that will evaporate it into nothingness. Beautiful trashless sky. Beautiful trashless space.

Or so I thought. I am proud of inventing the MV Pot-Belly Rocket which is now used by all countries. The poorer nations collaborate for rocket launches at centralized locations, but all collect for the purpose of a MV Pot-Belly Rocket launch. As launch costs continue to decrease over time, I foresee the day when each country can afford to do its own garbage disposal launches. Happy day! Beautiful trashless planet.

As someone obsessed with garbage disposal, I also founded the Museum of Trash Disposal which contains, among other things, garbage disposal methods during human history. I enjoy afternoon teas while watching old trash disposal videos, hence my distress over the 2016 Autocar Expeditor Labrie Expert 40/60 split body (video at https://www.youtube.com/watch?v=StQPNcL00-U). The truck gathers trash and recyclables from sidewalk bins colored black or gray for trash and blue for recyclable plastic, cardboard, and aluminum. The truck uses a forklift to lift the bins over the top of the truck which splits its container between garbage and recyclables. But garbage is often tipped into the recyclable part of its truck body and vice versa. Such adulterated contents drive me nuts. I'm so happy those days are behind us.

My MV Pot-Belly Rocket wouldn't work without a prior invention, the MV Gravitas Injection. This is chemical soup that we launch to inject into uninhabited space bodies like the huge rocks littering outer space. The injection penetrates the bodies and injects them with gravity (the name "Gravitas" is just a pun to amuse me). With gravity, the space bodies now can contain the garbage dumped onto it before it and its trash is obliterated.

I am recalling and sharing these details of my life and my inventions as I sit on an electric chair. My captors plucked the chair out of their review of human history to replicate as the tool for my death. Apparently, my captors admired its use for killing the rapists of Filipina actress Maggie de la Riva. Maggie's ordeal pioneered public discourse of rape in the Philippines. I heard these random facts when an ant explained why they chose this killing method. I think of the creature as an ant though I don't know what it is except that it is tiny. The creature and four others are on a matchstick-size piece of flotsam floating before my face.

Because the creatures are tiny, our survey of their planet overlooked their existence. So when we invaded it with human garbage and then blew it up, we apparently committed genocide. The five creatures were "out of town," as one put it, on a space exploratory mission and so were spared from our broklear bomb's decimation.

I begin to explain and apologize. "We tried to ensure we used only vacant space bodies...," I say before feeling an electric charge loosen my teeth and skew my lips into a momentary snarl. I comply with their unique order to be silent."For what it's worth," one ant communicates through inserting its thoughts into my brain, "we will spare your planet. We'll get rid of all humans, of course, before settling onto your planet to begin procreating."

I hear another ant laugh before it adds, "Trash will not be a problem. We're tiny, so our garbage is small. Your planet should be able to cope with our trash for a very long time."

I sigh and accept my fate. It's what I deserve for being a member of a species that practices heightism, the type of prejudice that privileges tall people as if they are more attractive, talented, intelligent and powerful. Too often, humanity has misunderstood matters of scale—there is no such thing as da Vinci's "Vitruvian Man." This and other prejudices should have been the garbage I'd addressed as an inventor. Instead, I'd accepted my 6'4" height as a deserved privilege and lived accordingly. No doubt there is justice for someone like me—human—being taken down by ants.

Letter to a Newly-Lapsed Nun & Other Philosophers

(An Epistolary Monobon)*

Dear _______________, [Fill in the blank]

Last night, I made love for the first time to my fiancé, Gregorio. I was the one who chose him, not my parents who preferred the neighbor's son attending med school, their friend's son who's successfully e-marketing whitening cosmetics, the son who'll inherit his parents' mining business, ... I could go on but nuff said on that. Dear _____________, I chose this man to marry because I wanted someone with an open mind as well as the self-confidence to have an open mind. The brain is a powerful sex organ, and I wanted to know my marriage would give me great sex! Like last night, when this happened:

Greggy shuddered. As I'd coaxed, his eyes stayed open like mine which never closes when I want to see what my actions birth. "I want to explore you," I whispered. "And I want to see everything you feel."

His torso arched as my tongue left his to travel and play elsewhere on his damp, salty body. His right nipple hardened between my fingers. I licked it, then softly blew over its newly plumped mound which heightened his moans. More licks. When I bit, he welcomed the pain as relief from my mouth's teasing. My left hand slipped under his warm back to heighten its arch as my tongue traveled to where another nipple waited. I was reminded of sweet golden raisins—how they're moister and more boxum than their cabernet-colored versions. But as I sucked, I also remembered the writer Steve Almond's tip of not likening nipples to Frankenstein's bolts while describing a sex scene. He spoke from experience after his lapse made him the beloved target of comedians.

Gregalicious whimpered as I moved my lips lower. My right hand was already inching to my next target. My tongue continued to descend, relishing each fleshly quiver. His chest wasn't chiseled into the "6-pack" preferred by my aunties who loved to gossip over the young men populating their teleseryes. But—if only because there'd be "more to love," as my slutty neighbor Rina liked to say about her tabachoy boyfriend—I've always preferred a hint of, if not the actual, beer belly on my lovers. It'd match the voluptuous "beer belly" on mine, courtesy of my favorite food, fatty kare-kare over steamed white rice with dollops of bagoong. *Oooooh, those kare-kare tuwalya sure look like spent manhoods after I spent them, but I digress…*

Anyway, I lifted my head from Gregorius's medium-plump belly to inspect my goal. *Ahh. A 10-percenter*, I observed with relish. I'd mostly experienced the more dominant structure displayed by 90% of humans. I wondered if Gregarino ever considered it—a belly button that stuck out as an "outie" instead of an "innie." Alternative spelling: "inny."

I don't discriminate against 10-percenters. Given the Onna-

Bugeisha within me, I appreciate how the scar pushed itself out to heighten its presence. Scars can be medals-of-honor, and the belly button is not, contrary to popular belief, the cut end of an umbilical cord—the belly button is scar tissue. As my tongue circled, my target hardened to become like a third nipple. Like one of Frankenstein's bolts. My mouth enclosed his scar, my tongue lapping at its tip that ended in the V-shaped proofreader's mark of a caret. To my pleasure, he shuddered.

As a child, I'd been obsessed with tales about the ancestor made possible by Japan's occupation of the Philippines in World War II. Decades later, when time diluted recriminations, my family focused on the familial history of our unwanted but undisputed relative—the Japanese soldier descended from a warrioress who'd helped form Japan's Female Warrior Golden Age. As skilled in combat as their male counterparts, they came into existence during the time of Empress Jingu, a Japanese empress who ruled as a regent following her husband's death in 200 CE.

Why then should I not be in control in anything I can control? I'd often thought after learning about my ancestor who'd excelled in the Naginata. The polearm was the iconic weapon of the Onna-Bugeisha, which literally means "female warriors."

The Naginata polearm. A polearm, my dear ____________, is a weapon whose blade is attached to the end of a long shaft. I may not have a penis, but I descend from a master wielder of a far-longer pole with devastating reach.

Sex is among the activities I prefer to control so that I can maximize my enjoyment of the scar that most ignore. Even when I rewarded my future husband by lowering my mouth further for that part of the body men prefer for receiving a woman's mouthy attention, my hands remained on his abdomen. My fingers continued to fondle his protruding belly button. Certain scars warrant caresses.

Later, I whispered, "Grazie, Leonardo" as I spooned him. One hand circled his chest so that my fingers could rest against his navel.

"Leonardo? My name is not Leonardo."

I regretfully released his Frankenstein bolt to soothe him by rubbing his belly. I nibbled at his ear lobe as I explained, "My Grigoli, I came to cherish belly buttons when I learned about da Vinci's Vitruvian Man. In drawing his concept of ideal proportions for the male human body, Leonardo centered his image on the navel. That's how my interest began, though it became a passion when I learned that the belly button is a scar."

Then I nudged Gregor's body to turn around. I preferred seeing my lover's face so I could monitor his expressions. "Scars resonate for me," I whispered between tiny licks at his lips. "Experience, then memory, forms us. Scars are memories. When we treasure someone, we should not ignore their scars. Scars form part of our identities."

I loved how he smiled easily, without judgement, and how his smile made his eyes shine. I loved it even more when he said, "I love how your mind works."

I lowered my right hand back down to his outie now between our bellies. As I stroked, Gryegori said. "Did you know that the oldest umbilical scar is from a 130-million-year-old dinosaur, the Psittacosaurus? Unlike reptiles and birds that lose their scars within days to weeks after hatching, its umbilicus persisted until sexual maturity. The Psittacosaurus gives us the oldest record of an amniote umbilicus and the first in a non-avian dinosaur."

Really? I was impressed and said so. "I'm impressed. Why would you know this factoid?"

Guregori grinned. "Because I wanted to impress you!" Laughing at my raised skeptical eyebrow, he said, "Okay. I wanted to please you. When I learned on our first date how, as you put it, belly buttons 'intrigue' you, I did some research. Of course, I didn't know then exactly how they intrigue you, but I'm delighted."

"I'm impressed," I said again," but also pleased. Thank you."

Gregorio deserved his name—it means "watchful" or "alert." If he loved me, that watchfulness would create acts of thoughtfulness, like his research into the navel. He pleased me so much I've looked for translations of his name in many languages: Grgo from Croatian, Geulegolio from Korean, Gligor from Romanian, Grega from Slovene, Krikor from Turkish, Gorgorios from Amharic, *Gregaaaaahhhhhh!* from when he made me come, and so on.

Gregorio turned to lay fully against the bed. He raised his hands behind his head and offered his naked body. His outie jutted out as robustly as his penis as he encouraged, "Do as you wish to do."

Do as I wish. Dear __________, this is what you want from a lover: encouragement to be yourself even if it means your partner must learn to accommodate, hopefully love, something new to them. Own your fetishes. Here's a poem mine inspired:

Outie

First, prepare:
Eat dark chocolate.
Cocoa increases blood
flow, which boosts
pleasure.

Tell a dirty joke:
"What did Cinderella
say to Prince Charming?"
[Insert Pause]
"Want to see if it fits?"

Next, you flirt:
Coo at it.
Blow gently over it.
A brief lick.
A longer, wetter lick.
Repeat.
Take your time: repeat.

Then you get down to it:
Part your lips.
Insert the tip
at the entrance
of your mouth.
Let your tongue
flicker at it.

Suck its entire length
inside your mouth.
Move your lips up
and down over it.

Your mouth has no
problem engulfing
it in its entirety.

Many men assume
the bigger the sexual
organ, the better
until they are taught
alvinophilia!

Scars reveal the biggest sex organ is the brain,

Eileen

** The "Epistolary Monobon" is a prose poetry form comprised of a letter whose sign-off is a monostich (one-line poem). Optionally, one can consider the letter to be the background to the monostich.*

Engraving 4

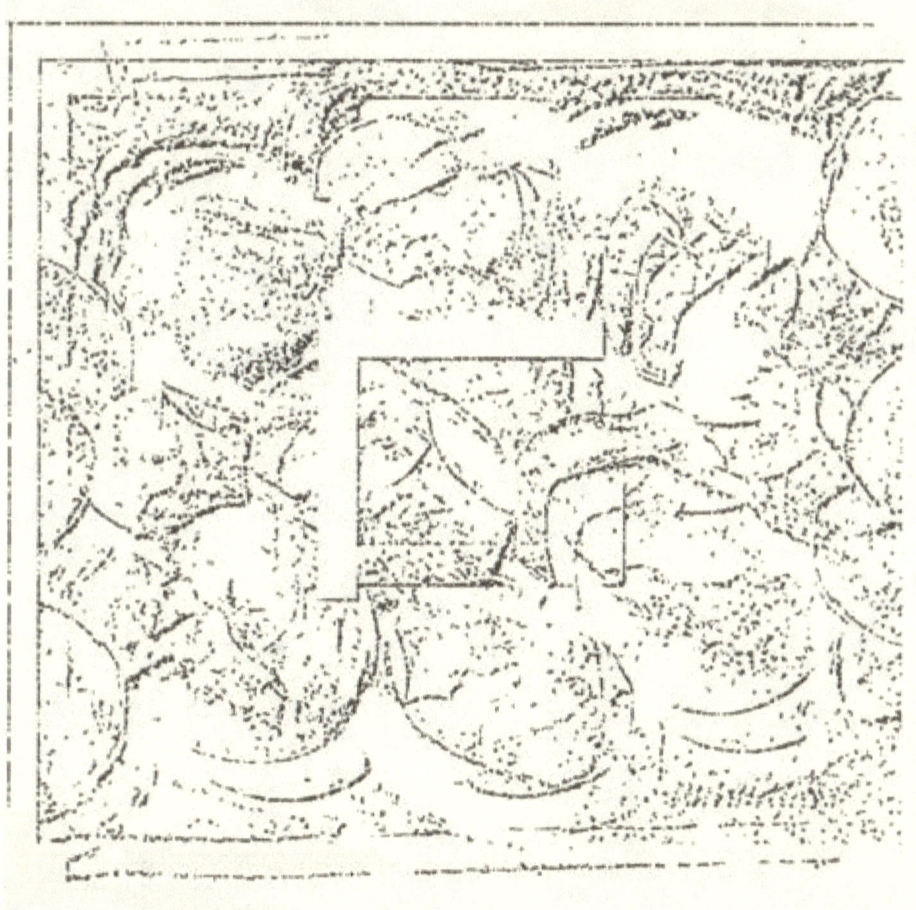

IV. ON POETRY

Truth is, so great
—Frida Kahlo

The First Poetry Book

She was young, and she was new to poetry.

Youth longs for difference. Youth longs for certain experiences simply because they're new.

She was new to poetry and felt exploring the unknown would be fruitful for creating poems. This camouflaged how she would have taken risks simply because she was young.

As a young poet, she wanted to write great poems even as she didn't yet know the meaning of greatness.

An older self would realize how we often cannot avoid behaving in response to forces indifferent to our well-beings. She was long before becoming that older self.

But her older self did not recall immediately the years she'd spent with him before choosing to enter Café Mandarin. The eatery made her pause on the sidewalk simply because she liked its red wooden door. It wasn't until she opened the door that she remembered that she'd once shared lunch with him at this small cafe. Since she'd already opened the door, she decided to enter.

She was greeted by a young woman whose not unfamiliar features made her mentally pause. Are you the child who used to sit silently in the corner of the room filling in the colors of your coloring book while your parents served the patrons? She remembered how she and he had enjoyed chatting with her after they were seated nearby. She had been proud of her just-colored picture of a butterfly with rainbow-colored wings flying away from a brown husk towards a blue sky. *It's just a useless cocoon!* the child had explained enchantingly when he'd asked about the brown blob.

The borderless, sunlit sky versus a quickly-withering cocoon that had outlived its purpose—*yes, youth longs for difference, for the new.*

She didn't divulge her thoughts to the woman leading her to her table. She merely said Thank You at the menu she offered after she sat down.

It's you!

When she raised her head at the exclamation from a patron at the next table, the past immediately intruded. In the years ahead, she occasionally would remember this moment of memory becoming present and marvel over how such a conflicted intrusion could surface so suddenly and unexpectedly with zero hesitancy.

It was he, older but still as discernible as the child who'd become her waitress. He was accompanied by his wife and daughter. The wife was the one who spoke, and he looked as startled as she felt.

You must be back in New York for NYU's poetry conference. Your lover is attending, too. She didn't raise her voice but its tone made her loathing clear.

Dear..., he turned to her just as she also uttered the same word to their daughter.

She looked at him with a scorn that silenced him. Dear, she repeated as she returned her gaze to their daughter. This is the woman who has the honor of being your father's last affair.

Their daughter looked at me, surprise dominating her violet eyes. Elizabeth Taylor, I thought uselessly as I considered how best to react to the unexpected situation then ensnaring me.

I looked away from them—from her. I didn't want to see the daughter's surprise transform into the same disgust in her mother's gaze. Or, worse, pain. From past online searches, she'd seemed to grow into a lovely person, in character as well as physically. She had turned aside a modeling then painting career to become an arts therapist at a juvenile detention center. He once said in a magazine article about poets' families that his daughter thinks it's more important that she uses art to help rehabilitate the future of incarcerated youth, rather than make her own paintings.

I remember nodding in agreement when I read his thought that she should have kept developing her own art because she actually showed great promise. The interview was illustrated with a photo of him seated beneath one of her early paintings, "Amorsolo." Though the painting features an eagle's head, the painting was titled after the Filipino painter because it explored what Fernando Amorsolo had mastered: sunlight.

I laid my menu on the table but before I could act further, her shadow dimmed the space. I turned to look at her looking down at me. Her lips quivered as her hands curled into fists. He was raising a hand towards her shoulder. It was an image that I realized I will never be able to forget—a young woman in pain and a father's hand attempting to move her away from the source of her anguish.

Then time ceased slowing and the mother was slapping away the father's hand so that she could be the one to draw her daughter away from me.

But she shook off her mother's hold and turned back to me. This time, anger had blackened her violet eyes. You knew he was married, and you went after him anyway. You're despicable.

I was despicable, yes, but I was young, I didn't reply.

Stop! She didn't quite scream at her parents still agitating behind her. But she gave the impression she would shout—*howl*, was the word that came to my mind—if they didn't let her engage me. They both froze to become mere backdrop to her then continuing to confront me.

Mom said you and my father continued your affair for over three years! Do you know how unhappy you made her?! Three years!

I stood so that I could give her the respect of facing her more directly than if I was seated. But I didn't speak so that she could continue her words. When aggrieved, the young rarely knew how to control their torrents of words unless it was with a complete, sullen silence.

Mom said it was your decision to stop your affair, not my father's! Here, she paused to toss a glare at her father before returning to me. Why did you even bother to end the affair?

So many more words. So many more stones hurled and I

felt each as if my body was glass. So many words that also mentioned how, once, her mother apparently attempted suicide shortly after she'd discovered her husband's betrayal. I remember when he told me about her suicide attempt and how that still hadn't stopped us that same afternoon from spending most of its hours wrecking our hotel bed. She finally stopped speaking after she repeated, Why did you even bother to end the affair?

At her question, I felt my age for the first time. I felt my spine curve a little. I felt tired. I looked at her damp face, still glowing despite her anger that was made more resonant by the tears she'd tried to dam but still leaked down her cheeks. I looked behind them and saw that the cafe had emptied itself of its other patrons. My waitress who I'd met as a young girl coloring a butterfly newly freed from her cocoon was nowhere in sight, perhaps hiding in the kitchen with her own shocked parents.

I felt tired but seriously considered her question as I picked up my bag and prepared to leave. There were two parts to the answer to her question. I knew I could only share one part. I said, I ended the affair when I heard your mother was pregnant with you. I knew he would absolutely love you, and I didn't want to interfere with that love.

She screamed then. What about my mother? You let her know about your affair for years! What about my mother?

I don't know, I thought. But what I know is that you've turned out as marvelously as I'd once hoped, even despite your mother choosing to reveal the news of your father's infidelity.

Surely it would have been more difficult if you had grown up with a father distracted by deceit from his paternal duties.

I picked up my bag and prepared to leave. Gently, I said, Your mother was equal to me.

To my relief, that silenced her. She seemed to freeze like her parents behind her.

As for him, he and I hadn't yet acknowledged each other. I wasn't surprised. We'd celebrated the first anniversary of our three-year relationship with a private dinner in a hotel suite reserved for the occasion. We'd swiftly depleted our first bottle of champagne. Of course, he opened a second bottle. As I watched him refill first his champagne flute, I realized that, someday, he and I would meet and feel only an indifference that would seem unimaginable given the passion we then shared, a passion so generative it would continue for what turned out to be another two years.

I began walking towards the exit. But I paused, my hand already on the bent brass knob but not yet opening the red door. I turned around to look at them. I saw a unity in their stance that I anticipated would strengthen as they would choose to grow into it. I realized then that the tableau they presented would be the fitting cover for my forthcoming first book of poetry which I'd titled *The Naked Flagpole*.

Before I met him, I'd often felt I hadn't yet experienced enough of life to write meaningful poems. Through him and the memories he helped me make, I created the poems in my first book that a future critic would deem worthy of trees being sacrificed for paper.

While I could not use their image formed just before I permanently left their world, the book's front cover would not be a far-fetched reminder. My book's cover will bear a reproduction of Frida Kahlo's 1936 painting, "My Grandparents, My Parents, and I." The oil on zinc and tempera painting, measuring 30.7 x 34.5 cm, represents the artist's family tree. Frida is depicted as a nude child holding a red ribbon to symbolize her family lineage. The ribbon matches the red cord to a fetus painted atop her mother's white dress as well as linked to the portraits of the artist's parents and both sets of grandparents.

I wished his family well. I wished Frida's family well. I wished all families well.

I was different. By choosing to birth poems, poems birthed me.

Afterword

"La Luna 'Before Silence of Winter Comes" appeared in *OurOwnVoice's Special Issue of Creative Works In Response to Other Works* (edited by Nadine Sarreal). A brief essay about the ekphrastic nature of my literary approach appeared with the story, and I share an excerpt below. While it specifically discusses one story, it generally exemplifies the approach underlying most of the stories in this collection:

<u>Introduction to "La Luna 'Before Silence of Winter Comes'"</u>

I love paintings. I find that paintings not only speak but are positively garrulous. While looking at a painting, I am often helpless against the urge to take a notepad and take dictation. My story "La Luna 'Before Silence Of Winter Comes'" is a tale containing sections that were dictated to me by the works of four artists: James Westwater, Jackson Pollock, Mark Rothko and Theresa Chong.

One of the characters, Jason Yardley, is described as a painter of works that "offered images of single lines curving across single-color backgrounds." These are the images I associate with a British artist I first met in New Mexico, James Westwater (not to be confused with a photographer of the same name). The first reference to Yardley's works in the story refers to some public criticism of his works, a reference that may seem negative towards the underlying inspiration: Westwater. But any implied criticism is purely fictional; I love Westwater's paintings, as evidenced partly by how I welcomed five of his works into my home.

I reference Yardley's/Westwater's images more positively later in the story when I mention how various line gestures on paintings are inspired by Jackson Pollock's figurative sketches, the other inspiration to the images I ascribe to Yardley. I offer Yardley saying, "He [Pollock] had this one gesture I recall from art school—something that's been popping up lately into my dreams. It was the way he drew the curve of a woman's breast, as if he could trace that arc forever. I want to evoke that passion with the lines I use to sunder solid blocks of color. If I must sunder, I must get lost in its movement!"

The painting referenced in the title—"La Luna Naranja"—is a work by the primary (unnamed) protagonist. "La Luna Naranja" is described as a containing an image of "the red-orange moon ... a circle whose edges touched four sides of the 68" X 68" canvas." The fictional painting was inspired by the large paintings of the lyrical colorist, Mark Rothko. In some of Rothko's works, one can see huge blocks of color pushing/expanding toward the edges of canvasses, just as I'd described for "La Luna Naranja."

Towards the end of the story, the primary character is described as having painted a series of black-and-white paintings. These fictional works were inspired by Theresa Chong. I once interviewed her and incorporated some technical details from that interview as regards the material for the paintings (e.g. not just generally paint but the specificity of Utrecht's non-yellowing white since it is the only white that doesn't yellow with age, that remains pure over time).

I also integrated what I'd learned about Chong's painting process: "The paintings were all sized at 20" X 20"—a scale that allowed me more intimacy than did my previous pieces. They were painted on board instead of canvas-specifically board which I'd first laid with gesso and then rigorously smoothened. After painting the surface white, I laid the board vertically against a wall. Using thin brushes dipped into black paint, I then dripped black paint from the top edge and allowed gravity to control how paint would flow down and create the linear pattern."

~~

It took decades for me to realize the significance of my Introduction's last paragraph to "La Luna 'Before Silence of Winter Comes'." Chong's black-and-white paintings can evoke a variety of elements, including how the paintings can recall vertical scrolls with Chinese (or other Asian) characters. This would mean that the artist created a visual artwork out of words. It seems fitting, then, that these artworks would inspire words through the letters of short stories.

—Eileen R. Tabios

Selected Notes & Bibliography

Ant-ish Lesson

Wikipedia on Maggie de la Riva

"The Undeserved Privilege of Height" by Aaron Limb, *The Ubiquity*, Feb. 7, 2023

The Art Collector

J. Paul Getty's and Agnes Gund's references are from *AT HOME WITH ART*, editors Estelle Ellis, Caroline Seebohm and Christopher Simon Sykes (Clarkson Potter Publishers, New York, 1999)

The reference to a Japanese billionaire who acquired a Van Gogh was inspired by the tales of Japanese paper mogul Ryoei Saito who paid $82.5 million for Van Gogh's portrait of Dr. Gachet and $78.1 million for Renoir's "Au Moulin de la Galette"

The reference to a bathroom scene was inspired by "Untitled #80 (Terra Cotta)," a photograph by Jeff Burton

Blue Richard

The story is partly inspired by the vortex imagery found in Native America pots and baskets as well as René Magritte's paintings of suspended elements such as "Golconda" and "The Castle of the Pyrenees"

Brutality

This is a reworked excerpt from Eileen R. Tabios' trunk novel, *Clandestine DNA*

The Caustic Surface

The author acknowledges Romare Bearden and Carl Holty for their book, *The Painter's Mind* (Crown Publishers, 1969) as well as Clinton Palanca whose story, "IDENTIFICATIONS," affected the sensibility of this story. Numbered footnotes refer to:

(1) from "Sui Veneris/The Poet Of No Return" by Ricardo M. De Ungria
(2) from "Insomnia" by Cassie Lewis
(3) from "Why I Wear My Hair Long" by Marilyn Kallet
(4) from "Saturn" by Norma Cole

(5) from "Biographies #2" by Eric Gamalinda
(6) from an interview of Ben Weber who responded to a question by Lou Harrison about the nature of composing with the reply, "I am moved to write music which seems inevitable..." (*Possibilities 1*, September 1947, edited by Robert Motherwell, Harold Rosenberg, Pierre Chareau and John Cage)
(7) from "Homunculi" by Eileen Tabios
(8) from "Forms of Politeness" by Mei-mei Berssenbrugge

The First Poetry Book

The story was inspired by a sentence in Katie Kitamura's wonderful novel *A Separation* (Riverhead Books, 2017) about how the young privilege new experiences

Information about the epigraphed Frida Kahlo quote is available at "To my Diego: 4 Poems by Frida Kahlo that Demonstrate the Exquisite Nature of Love" by Elyane Yousset, *Elephant Journal*, Oct. 19, 2016.

Information about Fernando Amorsolo is at https://www.lse.ac.uk/seac/events/2023/Fernando-Amorsolo-Master-Painter-of-Philippine-Sunlight-and-Elite-Conceptions-of-Nature

Information about Frida Kahlo's 1936 painting, "My Grandparents, My Parents, and I" is available at https://www.carredartistes.com/en-us/blog/mother-s-day-painting

La Luna "Before Silence of Winter Comes" and Afterword

"Helian," a poem by Austrian expressionist George Trakl, provided inspiration, including the line (which can vary depending on the English translation), "Before silence of winter comes." This powerful phrase also was integrated into the story's title. More information about George Trakl's poem "Helian" is available at https://talkaboutpoetry.wordpress.com/2016/04/01/trakl-helian/ and https://mypoeticside.com/poets/georg-trakl-poems

Letter to a Newly-Lapsed Nun & Other Philosophers

The "Epistolary Monobon is a variation of the poetry form

"monobon" conceived by Eileen R. Tabios to be prose ending with a monostich. More information on the form is available at https://eileenrtabios.com/projects/monobon/

"Outie"'s dirty joke is from "105 Dirty Jokes That Will Definitely Make You Blush" by Morgan McMurrin, *Parade*, June 8, 2024

Non-Fungible Armadillo Shells
"NFTs, explained" by Mitchell Clark, *The Verge*, June 6, 2022
"Beeple sold an NFT for $69 million" by Jacob Kastrenakes, *The Verge*, March 11, 2021
"Top 15 Cheap Vodka Brands That Won't Break the Bank" by Paul Kushner, *My Bartender*, February 2023

One Eye Open
"50+ Weird but True Facts That Will Blow Your Mind" by Julie Sprankles, *Scary Mommy*, April 29, 2021. Wikipedia on dolphins

Polmost Spirytus Rektyfikowany Vodka
"Artist rediscovers mysterious recipe for ancient 'Maya Blue' dye" by Mark Viales, *Mexico News Daily*, March 14, 2023

Red "Afterbirth"
The story is dedicated to some visual artists I met at the Virginia Center for the Creative Arts: Ann Cooper, Mindy Bellof and Suzanne Adams; and written in homage to Richard Tuttle's Sculptures of String, Pencil, Wall, Shadow, Space and Optics

The phrases *"I forgot the horizon is far, is near, is what you wish but always in front of you. / I forgot one can choose always to face the horizon"* are from *Murder Death Resurrection* by Eileen R. Tabios (Dos Madres Press, 2018)

The prose paragraph excerpt at the end of the story is from the author's poem "Homunculi"

Acknowledgements

Deep thanks to my visual artist collaborator harry k stammer and publisher Sandy Press (editors Mark Young and harry k stammer). I'm also grateful to those who've supported various aspects of this project over the past three decades: Gloria Rodriguez, Jean Vengua, Bino A. Realuyo, Alfred "Krip" Yuson, Greg Brillantes, Reme Grefalda, Nadine Sarreal, D. Hideo Maruyama, Richard Peabody, August Highland, Anselm Berrigan, harry k stammer, Mark Young, Thomas Fink, Sandy McIntosh, Rupert Loydell, Ninotchka Rosca, Jean Vengua and Marianne Villanueva. Salamat as well to the following organizations who provided artist residences for writing some of the stories: Virginia Center for the Creative Arts, the MacDowell Arts Colony and Fundacion Valparaiso (Spain).

The following publications first published (earlier versions of) these stories:

The Brooklyn Rail: "One Eye Open," "Polmost Spirytus Rektyfikowany Vodka," and "Non-Fungible Armadillo Shells"
Café Bellas Artes: "Einstein's Love Story"
*Dis*Orient*: "Red 'Afterbirth'"
Gargoyle: "The Artist Looks at the Model"
International Times: "Bar-Hopping Sentences"
The Literary Review: "The 'Other'"
Muse Apprentice Guild: "About Face"
OurOwnVoice (Special Issue on Creative Works In Response to Other Works): "La Luna 'Before the Silence of Winter Comes'"
Philippine Graphic: "Einstein's Love Story"
Wordwrights!: "Einstein's Love Story"

"Blue Richard" was previously published in *The Nuyorasian Anthology*, editor Bino A. Realuyo (Temple University Press, 1999).

"Red Afterbirth" was previously published in the "Love Stories Series" at Cecilia Brainard Blog, 2025.

"Bar-Hopping Sentences" was written for Marianne Villanueva for calling each story's opening sentence of my short story collection, *Getting to One*, "such a winner."

"Letter to a Newly-Lapsed Nun & Other Philosophers" was written for Ninotchka Rosca.

Earlier versions of some stories were previously published in the author's prose/art collaboration with visual artist harry k stammer *Getting to One* (Sandy Press, 2023) and the author's out-of-print book *Behind the Blue Canvas* (Giraffe Books, 2004).

About the Writer and Artist

Eileen R. Tabios has released books of poetry, fiction, art and experimental prose from publishers around the world. Recent releases include the poetry collections *Engkanto in the Diaspora* and *Because I Love You, I Become War*; a novel *The Balikbayan Artist*; an art monograph *Drawing Six Directions*; an autobiography, *The Inventor: A Poet's Transcolonial Autobiography*; and fiction/art collaborations with harry k stammer, *Getting To One* and *The Erotic Space Around Objects*. Other books include a first novel *DoveLion: A Fairy Tale for Our Times* which was translated by Danton Remoto into Filipino as *KalapatingLeon* and two French poetry books, *PRISES (Double Take)* (trans. Fanny Garin) and *La Vie erotique de l'art* (trans. Samuel Rochery). In 2027, she will release a book combining a poetry collection and a novel, *Collateral Damage Blues*. Her body of work includes invention of the hay(na)ku, a 21st century diasporic poetic form; the MDR Poetry Generator that create poems totaling theoretical infinity; the "Flooid" poetry form that's rooted in a good deed; and the monobon poetry form based on the monostich. Translated into 13 languages, she has seen her writing and editing works receive recognition through awards, grants and residencies. More information is at https://eileenrtabios.com

harry k stammer is a writer, musician and painter who lives and works in Santa Barbara, CA USA. His books include *every beyond't nothing* (persistencia), *tents* (Otoliths), *grounds* (Otoliths); and *tocsin* (Otoliths), *sidewalkss* (Concrete Mist Press), *walls't's* (Sandy Press), *-48* (Sandy Press), *alleys't'* (Concrete Mist Press), *gravel* with Mark Young and Mark Cunningham, *gutter 's* (Sandy Press) and *haui-qt seared.* Recent noise/poetry pieces are available at http://harrykstammer.bandcamp.com

www.ingramcontent.com/pod-product-compliance
Lightning Source LLC
LaVergne TN
LVHW090517110826
845146LV00003B/889

* 9 7 9 8 9 9 2 4 5 8 2 9 9 *